The world of computers brought to life before your eyes!

W9-ARX-096

ROAD RALLY!

Programming Illustrated shows you in full color:

- What happens when a computer program runs

- How a programmer writes a Windows application

- Why a program works like it does

- How DOS, Windows, OS/2, and Mac programming differ

- What loops, clauses, and instructions are

Upgrading Your PC Illustrated shows you in full color:

- How to upgrade a computer's processor and memory

- What's needed to install a disk drive, modem, or sound card

- How to add a mouse, printer, game port, or video system

- How DOS, Windows, OS/2, and Mac programming differ

- What loops, clauses, and instructions are

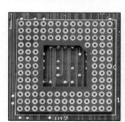

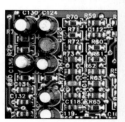

COMPUTERS
ILLUSTRATED

Written by
Nat Gertler

Designed by
Amy Peppler-Adams

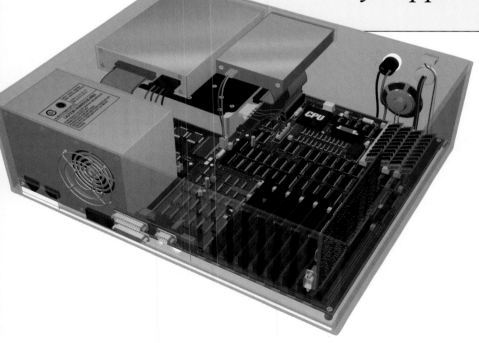

que

Computers Illustrated

Library of Congress Catalog No.: 94-65331

ISBN: 1-56529-676-1

97 96 95 94   4 3 2 1

Interpretation of the printing code: the rightmost double-digit number is the year of the book's printing; the rightmost single-digit number, the number of the book's printing. For example, a printing code of 94-1 shows that the first printing of the book occurred in 1994.

Publisher: David P. Ewing

Associate Publisher: Michael Miller

Publishing Director: Joseph B. Wikert

Managing Editor: Michael Cunningham

Marketing Manager: Greg Wiegand

CREDITS

Publishing Manager
Brad R. Koch

Acquisitions Editor
Angie Lee

Product Director
Robin Drake

Production Editor
Thomas F. Hayes

Technical Editor
Jerry L. Cox

Acquisitions Coordinator
Patricia J. Brooks

Cover Designers
Dan Armstrong
Amy Peppler-Adams

Illustrators
Michael Buck
David Cripe
Dennis Ladigo
Shelly Norris
Anthony StuART

Illustration Art Director
Rich Whitney

Production Team
Jeff Baker
Claudia Bell
Cameron Booker
Anne Dickerson
Karen Dodson
Teresa Forrester
Joelynn Gifford
Bob LaRoche
Andrea Marcum
Tim Montgomery
Caroline Roop
Dennis Sheehan
Sue VandeWalle
Mary Beth Wakefield
Kelli Widdifield

Composed in *New Baskerville* and *MCPdigital* by Que Corporation.

DEDICATION

I would like to dedicate this book to every woman who ever seriously kissed me, if only because by making such a dedication, I might encourage other women to do the same.

ABOUT THE AUTHOR

"Nat Gertler is the best-selling author of Computers Illustrated" is how he would like his next biography to start off. Nat is perhaps the first full-blooded second generation computer programmer, as both of his parents were computer programmers before his birth. In addition to his programming career, Nat has written for books, magazines, television, and even comic books, where he has chronicled the adventures of everyone from Speed Racer to Santa Claus. His supposed free time is spent performing with comedy troupe Doorways To Lint, searching for women to kiss, and writing about himself in the third person. He lives in Hi-Nella, New Jersey, with far too many floppy disks and far too few labels for them.

ACKNOWLEDGMENTS

A book like this is not easy to give birth to, and if I am its proverbial mother (a bearded mother though I may be) then there are a multiple of wonderful and helpful uncles without whom it would not have been possible or worthwhile.

The Fine Uncles at Que

Many uncles in the Que family have earned my thanks: Uncle Tom Hayes pushed me for more detail, Uncle Jerry Cox pointed out when I was less than precise, and Uncle Robin Drake caught places where I was less than clear and let me know that the whole thing worked. Then there's Uncles Angie Lee and Patty Brooks, for the patience and hard work that they put into this crazy project. More than any others, however, I owe thanks to Uncle Brad Koch, for believing that a combination computer programmer/comic book writer was the right author for this book, for giving me the basic structure of the book, and for being flexible when I wanted to reshape the book based on my own vision.

The Art Uncles

Big thanks to the crew at Accent Technical Communications for taking my refrigerator-quality doodles and turning them into the amazingly rendered images that fill these pages. Kudos to Uncle Rich Whitney and Uncle Cathy Winkler for pushing their staff hard to get the vast amount of material out on time without sacrificing quality.

The illustrations, color renderings, and 3-D modeling in this book were produced by Michael Buck, Dennis Ladigo, David Cripe, Michael Steiner, Anthony Stuart, and Craig Thurmond of Accent Technical Communications, an Indianapolis-based company. Accent's staff of 45 professionals include illustrators, writers, page composers, programmers, and engineers who produce high-quality text and graphics for printed publications. Accent also does computer animation, interactive multimedia presentations, database publishing of industrial catalogs, and CD-ROM production.

Also, thanks to Uncle Ted Slampyak, who has worked with me before yet still was willing to draw the silly picture of me that graces my bio.

Uncles of Knowledge

While this might seem cliché, a large amount of thanks is really due to Uncle Mom and Uncle Dad, both of whom have taught me much about computers, and both of whom helped create a home environment where the computer was a standard tool. There have been many other teaching uncles over the years, whether at Simon's Rock College, Avant-Garde Computing/Boole and Babbage Network Systems, or as members of user groups and bulletin board systems. Then there are the countless authors of books and magazine articles who have kept me up-to-date with this ever-changing world of high technology. A special tip of the hat to the uncle-like folks on the CompuServe Comics Forum, because without their interesting conversation, I would not have been around to get involved with this project.

But last of all, I would like to express my own bizarre affection for all of the many computers I have owned or operated over the past 16 years, each of which taught me something—usually by breaking down and requiring me to poke around its innards, but that's just a computer's way of getting your attention. They're digital uncles, one and all.

TRADEMARK ACKNOWLEDGMENTS

All terms mentioned in this book that are known to be trademarks or service marks have been appropriately capitalized. Que cannot attest to the accuracy of this information. Use of a term in this book should not be regarded as affecting the validity of any trademark or service mark. Trademarks indicated below were derived from various sources.

Lotus, and 1-2-3 are registered trademarks of Lotus Development Corporation.

Ami Pro is a trademark of Lotus Development Corporation.

Microsoft Windows is a trademark of Microsoft Corporation.

DeskJet and LaserJet are registered trademarks of Hewlett-Packard Company.

WordPerfect is a registered trademark of WordPerfect Corporation.

CONTENTS

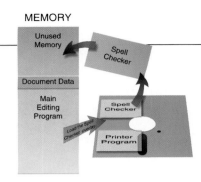

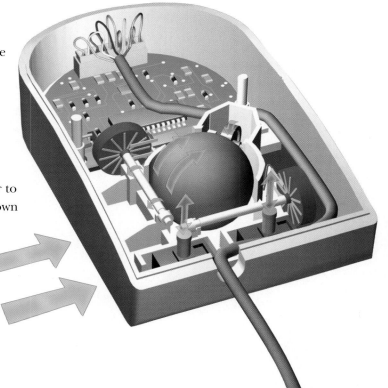

INTRODUCTION

INTRODUCTION

Welcome to *Computers Illustrated*! This book is designed to give you a lot of information about how your computer works. You'll learn about things like *megabits* and *system buses* and *double-spin CD-ROMs*.

Computers are a lot like cars. You don't have to understand that much about what's going on under the hood in order to drive a car to the supermarket. However, when it comes time to buy a car, or should something go wrong with it, it really pays to understand what the carburetor does. Similarly, when you want to buy computer equipment, or when the computer behaves in a way that you did not expect (and it will), understanding what goes on inside the computer will help you immensely.

You don't need to have any technical background in order to understand anything in this book. The information that you need to know is displayed in large pictures and clear diagrams. This will help you grasp instantly what is being discussed.

The first column on each spread provides background information for the topic being illustrated on that spread.

What Happens When You Use Your Scanner?

The most affordable scanners are hand scanners. These are simple, hand-held devices which are dragged across the page you wish to scan.

Because of this, the clarity of the image depends to a degree on the smoothness and steadiness of the dragging motion. Newer models make a straight, smooth drag easier, and perform better when the drag isn't smooth.

Flatbed scanners automate the process—making smoother scans—and can scan a full page at a time. They cost more but, for those with more than casual scanning needs, are generally worth the added cost.

HAND SCANNERS AND FLATBED SCANNERS

The light bounces off a mirror.

The light is reflected off the paper. Dark areas on the paper reflect less light.

A bright light is shined on the page.

The flatbed scanner appears to be very much like a photocopier, with a glass plate, a cover, and a light bar which slides down the length of the page. Its internal workings, however, are very much like that of the hand scanner.

188

In addition to the main illustration, there may be smaller illustrations adding further depth to the topic at hand.

Every spread has one large illustration, which gives you an image of the item being discussed and lets you see how it fits into the computer's overall operation.

FACTS

Not every section has a Facts column. If the section's topic can be explained with the pictures and the background column, it will be left at that.

Sections that are longer than two pages will have the background information on the first spread and the facts information (if any) on the last.

New terms that appear on the spread are in a different color. The glossary in the back of the book provides definitions of these important terms that appear throughout the book. They will direct you to the proper section of the book for more detailed information. Likewise, the Table of Contents in the front of the book will lead you in the proper direction.

What Happens When You Use Your Scanner?

FACTS

Scanners are rated by two factors: the size of the grid that they break the image into, and how many different shades those dots can be.

The grid size is measured in dots per inch. Usually, a single number refers to both the horizontal and vertical measurements.

The number of shades on a non-color scanner is referred to as the gray scale. It will be a power of 2 (256, for example), since a fixed number of bits will be used.

Color resolution is referred to by the number of bits or the total number of colors those bits can represent (8-bit color is the same as 256 colors).

Just because your scanner uses a high resolution doesn't mean that you'll be able to take full advantage of it. For example, if you scan a 4-inch-by-4-inch photograph with a 256 gray scale setting, then you are generating 5 megabytes worth of data. While some compression can be done, this still may be too much data for your system to easily handle. High-powered graphic work calls for a system with a lot of RAM, and fills up a lot of disk space.

ocuses the light ensor array.

This bank of light sensors detects the level of reflected light.

The hand scanner is on a roller that is connected by gears to a slotted wheel. This wheel works just like the one inside an opti-mechanical mouse to track the speed and distance of the scanner's motion.

Red Separation

Green Separation

Blue Separation

Both flatbed and hand scanners are available that handle color. They separately measure the amount of red, green, and blue light reflected, and the program combines that into a single image.

189

The last column on each spread displays additional information about this aspect of the computer. This column includes items that are particularly interesting or informative, but go beyond what is covered in the pictures. A lot of technical jargon is explained here.

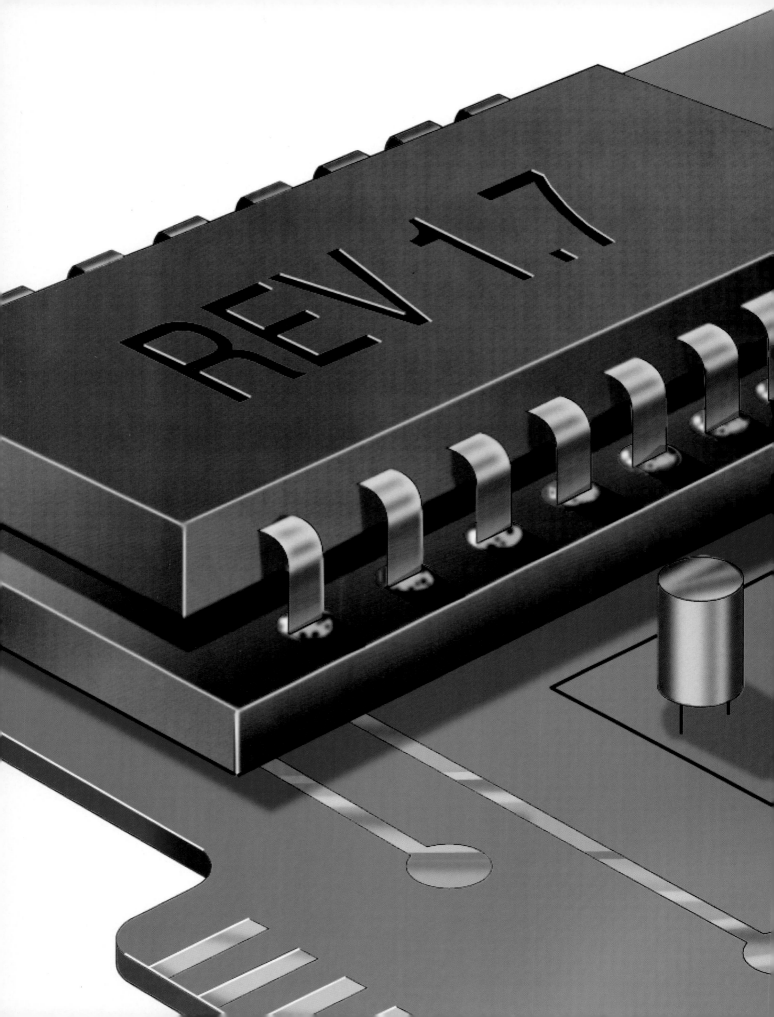

CHAPTER

1

WHAT IS A COMPUTER?

WHAT IS A COMPUTER?

A personal computer can do a lot more than a watch can, but the concept is still the same—it's still just an information appliance. It takes input, processes it in some way, and creates output.

It's easy to point at the box sitting on your desk and say "this is a computer." But what do we mean by computer? A computer is an information appliance.

A toaster is a food appliance. You put bread into it, and you get toast. With a computer, information is put in, and information comes out. The information you put in (called input) can include data and commands. Data is the facts that you want the computer to process. Commands tell the computer what sort of processing to do with the data. The information you get from a computer is called output.

A digital watch is a simple computer. The output is the current time and date. This information is based on the data that you put in when you set a watch—the starting time and date. By pressing a little button, you give the watch commands to show you the time or the date. The watch is processing the input by constantly updating the time and date, and displaying whichever you request in numbers on the LCD.

FACTS

Input, processing, and output don't have to take place in a neatly separated order. When you play a video game (which is a type of computer), for example, you are constantly giving input—the joystick movements indicate which direction you want to go. The video game computer is constantly taking that input, processing it to figure out where you are on-screen, whether or not you have run into anything, what your score is, and things like that. The computer also is constantly providing output—the screen display which shows where you are, where everything else is, and the score.

This book focuses on the family of personal computers that starts with the IBM PC and continues with computers from other manufacturers (often referred to as IBM compatibles). However, many of the concepts described here apply equally as well to the entire range of computers—from digital watches all the way up to the modern super computer.

The word *data* is actually plural, meaning *pieces* of information. The singular, meaning a single piece of information, is datum. Most people these days use *data* for both singular and plural, though, and it has come to be accepted.

Computer output comes in many forms. The computer can display information on-screen, or print it out on a printer. It also can pass information to other computers via a modem or a network. It can store information on a disk or a tape, so that it (or another computer) can use that information as input at another time.

A personal computer gets input from many sources. It can get both data and commands from users typing on the keyboard, or from a computer disk. It also can get input from scanners, modems, and networks, among other sources.

ALL INFORMATION IS NUMERIC

The heart of the computer is designed around math and math-type logic. In order to be able to deal with information, the computer must reduce it to numbers. Letters get turned into numbers. Pictures get turned into lists of numbers. The method for translating these things into numbers differs, depending on what is being translated.

Because of this number orientation, the computer is much better at numerical tasks than it is at handling things that deal with abstract concepts. The computer's ability to handle abstract concepts is dependent upon the ability of the computer programmer to reduce those concepts into numeric concepts the computer can handle. That's why a computer can be programmed to play a good game of chess (with its rigid format and limited ways of moving a limited number of pieces, chess is easy to represent mathematically). But a computer would be lousy at an abstract game like charades, because recognizing a simple concept like "sounds like" is difficult for a computer, much less trying to recognize meaning in a wide range of hand gestures.

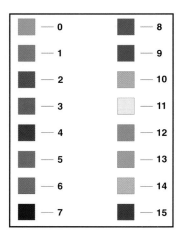

Each individual color in the limited color set (or palette) is represented by a specific number.

— 0		— 8	
— 1		— 9	
— 2		— 10	
— 3		— 11	
— 4		— 12	
— 5		— 13	
— 6		— 14	
— 7		— 15	

A drawing would seem to be a very difficult thing to describe in terms of numbers, but computers deal with drawings all the time. Instead of dealing with a picture as smooth lines and infinite subtle variations in colors, the computer reduces the picture to a grid of boxes, each one a single color from a limited set of colors.

FACTS

Even when the computer deals with text information, it treats each character of the text as a number.

The system usually used for encoding text is called ASCII (short for American Standard Code for Information Interchange, and rhymes with *passkey*). This code has a different number set aside for each uppercase letter, each lowercase letter, each punctuation mark, and so on. For example, the ASCII version of

    Hello!

would be

    72 101 108 108 111 33

The two 108s stand for the two ls.

Because ASCII is used as a standard by so much of the computing world, it makes it easier to transport information between programs, and even between different computer systems.

0	2	3	3	5	0	1	5	2	3
0	3	6	3	5	0	0	2	11	13
0	2	3	5	2	0	1	5	5	5
1	4	2	5	3	1	6	6	6	2
0	3	3	5	6	8	8	8	8	8
0	2	2	7	6	8	8	8	8	8
1	5	5	5	6	9	8	9	10	10
1	4	2	4	2	8	8	11	12	12
1	2	2	2	2	9	9	13	9	9
1	4	2	5	6	8	9	13	9	9

By translating each color to that color's number on the palette list, the computer ends up with a grid of numbers that it uses internally to represent the picture.

A s you just learned, computers handle everything as numbers. Human beings have a counting system based on the number 10, probably because we have ten fingers. This system is called decimal or base 10. We can count with one digit until we get to 9. To represent ten, we have to start a second column, where we keep track of the number of tens. Using these two columns, we can count up to 99—then we start another column to keep track of multiples of the next largest number, 100. By stringing together enough digits that are each 0 through 9, you can represent numbers as large as you want.

A computer, however, doesn't have fingers, so a counting system based on 10 doesn't make sense for it. What it has instead is a bunch of little switches, called bits. (These bits are the machine's way of holding information.) Each switch must be either on or off. One position (off) stands for the number 0, the other position (on) stands for 1. Because each bit is a single digit, 1 or 0, you can't count up to 9 with one digit—only to 1. Still, with enough of these one-bit digits strung together, the computer can represent numbers as large as it needs. This system for representing a number as a series of 1s and 0s or on and off switches is called binary or base 2.

WHAT ARE BINARY NUMBERS?

1

2   1

With just one column, a "ones" column, we can have the switch set to 0, indicating that the value being stored is zero, or we can set it to 1, indicating that the value being stored is one. Once we get above 1, we have to start another column.

The next column is the "twos" column. To count to 2 in binary, the computer uses a 1 in the "twos" column $(1 \times 2=2)$ and a 0 in the "ones" column $(0 \times 1-0)$. If we have a 1 in each column (11 binary), we have $(1 \times 2=2)+(1 \times 1=1)$, or 3. To get above that, we need to add another column, which will be the "fours" column, so that we can represent numbers 4 and above.

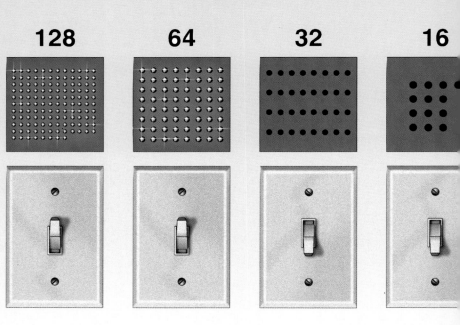

128   64   32   16

With a "fours" column, we can count from 100 binary (which is 4 in decimal) up to 111 binary (or 7 decimal—4+2+1). Then we have to add an "eight's" column to handle numbers above that, and so on.

All the bits in the computer's memory and processing equipment are gathered in groups of eight. A group of eight bits is called a byte. *With a single byte, any value from 0 through 255 can be represented in binary. In the example pictured, the byte (11000100 binary) represents 128+64+4, or 196. When the computer needs to deal with numbers in a range greater than 0 to 255, it starts using multiple bytes. With two bytes, for example, it can represent any number from 0 to 65,535.*

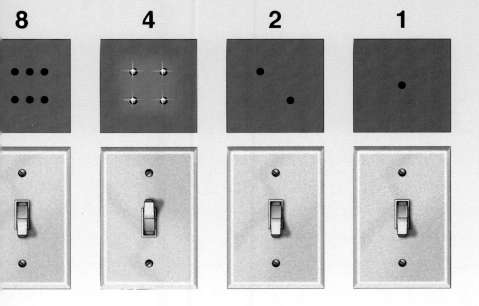

FACTS

Notice that there is a pattern to the values of the different bits. After 1, there's 2, and then there's 4, which is 2 × 2. Then there is 8, which is 2 × 2 × 2, and 16, which is 2 × 2 × 2 × 2, and so on. Computers tend to like exact powers of 2. That there are *eight* bits in a byte, rather than 7 or 10, is an example of this.

Programmers like to deal with something they call hexadecimal—or hex—when keeping track of numbers relating to the computer's internal workings. This is because when you write numbers in binary, they just end up being a long string of 0s and 1s, which are a pain to type and all too easy to make mistakes with. Instead, the programmers break each byte into two sets of 4 bits apiece, and translate each set to a single character, based on the following chart:

Binary	Hex	Binary	Hex
0000	0	1000	8
0001	1	1001	9
0010	2	1010	A
0011	3	1011	B
0100	4	1100	C
0101	5	1101	D
0110	6	1110	E
0111	7	1111	F

So when a programmer talks about a value of 3B hex, it's the same as 00111011 binary, or 59 decimal.

BINARY LOGIC

All the calculating equipment inside a computer is based on binary logic. The electronic machinery it takes to understand each possible command is made up of several calculations based on just two bits apiece. By taking the results of each little calculation and using it to build the next one, very complex calculations and commands are possible.

In order to understand these calculations, it is easiest to think of our little bit switches as switching between "true" and "false," rather than 1 and 0. Then we can look at the building blocks of binary logic, and see that it is very much like logic that people use all the time.

It's Saturday

TRUE

FALSE

It's Sunday

TRUE

FALSE

OR

It's the weekend

TRUE

FALSE

The logical operator OR checks the two bits coming in, and as long as they aren't both *false, it puts out a "true" result. If either "It's Saturday" or "It's Sunday" is true, then the statement "It's the weekend" is true.*

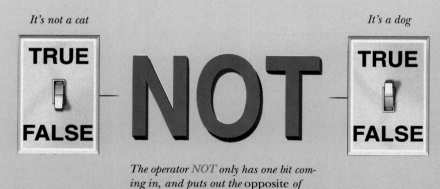

It's not a cat

TRUE

FALSE

NOT

It's a dog

TRUE

FALSE

The operator NOT only has one bit coming in, and puts out the opposite *of whatever that bit is. If a "true" bit is put in, a "false" bit comes out. If a "false" bit is put in, a "true" bit comes out. If your pet is* either *a dog or cat, this logic determines which type of pet you have.*

FACTS

In addition to the operators AND, OR, and NOT, binary logic also uses operators called NAND, NOR, and XOR. But these operators can be made by linking together ANDs, ORs, and NOTs. (Electronically, NOR and NAND are actually *simpler* circuits than OR and AND.)

The NAND operator (short for "not and") gives a false result only if both bits going in are true.

The NOR operator (short for "not or") gives a true result only if both bits are false.

The XOR operator (short for "exclusive or") puts out a true result if the two bits going in are different, and a false result if they are both the same (either both true or both false).

It's Friday

The logical operator AND puts out a "true" result only when both of the bits being checked are true. Because it's not Friday, it can't be Friday the 13th.

It's Friday the 13th

It's the 13th

WHAT IS A COMPUTER PROGRAM?

A program is simply a list of commands that tell the computer how to perform a task. The commands tell it where to take the input from, how to process it, and what kind of output goes where.

Some computers, like the one in a digital watch, have all of their programs built-in. You cannot change the program to make the watch do anything but tell time. The only commands that you can give the watch are the few that the built-in program was designed to understand.

Personal computers, however, are designed to let you put in different programs. Just like a VCR can act as a movie theater, an aerobics instructor, or an album of photos of your grandchild (depending on what tape you put into it), a computer can perform many different tasks depending on the programs you install. When you use a word processing program, the computer becomes a word processor. When you use a game program, it becomes a game machine.

A computer program can be very complex, often involving hundreds of thousands of individual commands. The computer only understands a limited (but useful) set of commands, and difficult procedures have to be broken into long strings of these small steps.

NIGHT-TIME:
Sleep until you wake up.

WAKING UP:
If the alarm clock isn't ringing yet, leap back to NIGHT-TIME routine.
If it's SATURDAY or SUNDAY, leap ahead to WEEKEND routine.
Turn off alarm clock.
Eat breakfast.
Go to work.
Work.
Come home from work.
Eat dinner.
Watch sitcoms.
Leap back to NIGHT-TIME routine.

WEEKEND:
Eat breakfast.
Go for a bike ride.
Eat lunch.
Watch sports.
Eat dinner.
Watch more sports.
Leap back to NIGHT-TIME routine.

When a program is used, not all of the commands are executed in the order that they are in the list. Some of the commands tell the computer to jump around the list. If you were to program yourself to live your life, the command list might look something like this.

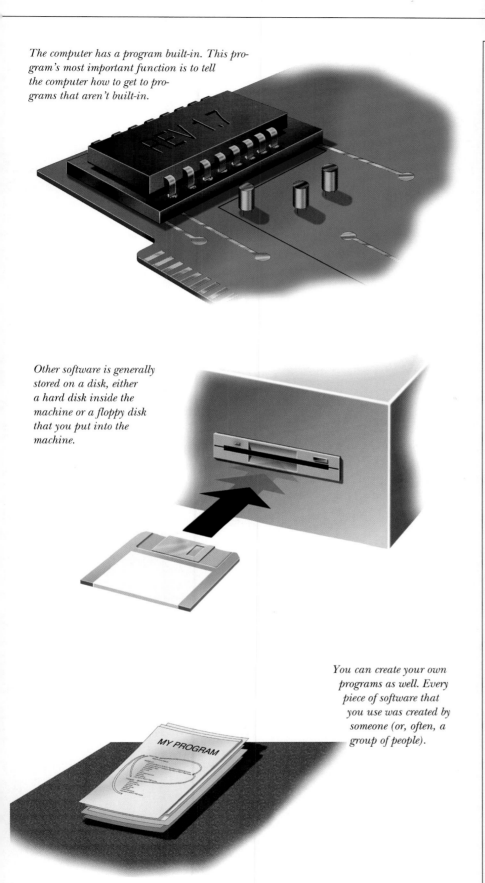

The computer has a program built-in. This program's most important function is to tell the computer how to get to programs that aren't built-in.

Other software is generally stored on a disk, either a hard disk inside the machine or a floppy disk that you put into the machine.

MY PROGRAM

You can create your own programs as well. Every piece of software that you use was created by someone (or, often, a group of people).

FACTS

People who create computer programs (programmers) rarely do so in the language that the computer directly understands (machine language). Machine language commands are nothing but numbers. Instead, programmers write in programming languages designed for this task. This allows them to work in a way that is more understandable to them.

These programs are then translated by another program into a form that the computer can directly handle. These translation programs, called compilers, assemblers, and interpreters, break the big steps of the programming language into the smaller, numeric steps that the computer understands.

Compilers and assemblers translate the program into machine language and save the machine language version on disk.

An interpreter handles each of the programmer's commands one at a time, translating it into the smaller commands the machine understands, and then immediately acting on those commands. Because it is trying to translate the program as well as act on the commands every time the program is used, this is slower than using a program that has been translated ahead of time by a compiler or an assembler.

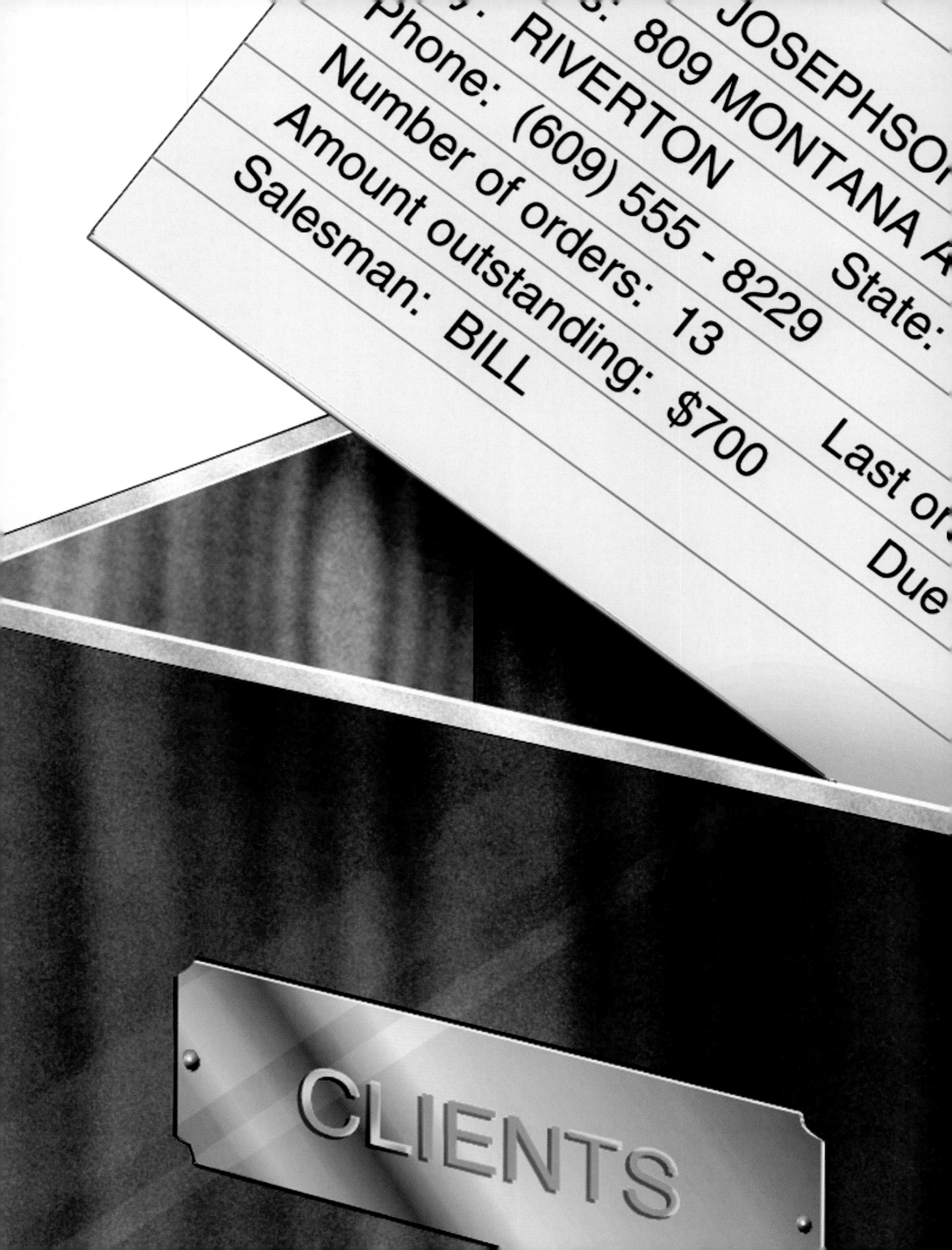

JOSEPHSO
s: 809 MONTANA A
y: RIVERTON
State:
Phone: (609) 555 - 8229
Number of orders: 13
Amount outstanding: $700   Last or
Salesman: BILL   Due

CLIENTS

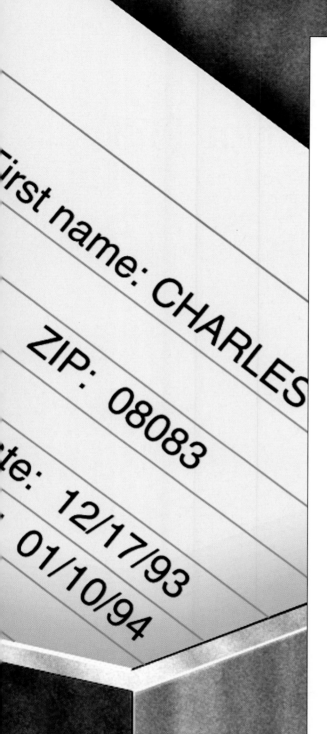

First name: CHARLES

ZIP: 08083

te: 12/17/93

01/10/94

2

WHAT CAN A COMPUTER DO FOR ME?

Word Processing

Desktop Publishing

Keeping Records

Doing Math

Painting and Drawing

Telecommunications

Games

WHAT CAN A COMPUTER DO FOR ME?

If you have flipped through this book already (admit it, you have!), you have seen that it's mostly about how a computer does what it does. While looking so hard at what a computer is doing internally, it's easy to lose track of what the computer is doing for you. If these amazing machines aren't serving you in some way, then they have no purpose.

The computer can do a lot of things for you. It's easily the most versatile new tool since the discovery of the stick. That's because every computer program turns the same piece of equipment into a brand new tool—and there are literally thousands of different programs. Many programs duplicate things that we do without computers, only allowing us to do them faster and better. Other programs help us to do things that would not be possible without computers. The computer is the central element on the modern desk because it replaces most of the items that used to be on the desk.

A computer isn't just for work, either. The personal and entertainment uses are endless.

In this chapter, we look at some of the most common types of computer programs, and what they can do to make your life easier and better.

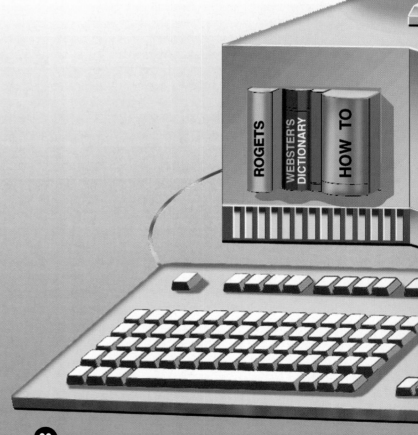

A-C

WORD PROCESSING

Writing any kind of document—a letter, a report, or a story—is tricky at best. Many bad decisions and mistakes can be made along the way. When working on a typewriter, making changes is difficult, and generally requires retyping a large amount of work.

Word processing programs allow you to compose your writing in the computer's memory and change it any way you want before committing it to paper. Even once you print the writing, it's still stored in the computer, so you can go back and make changes without retyping the whole thing.

With a word processing program, you type as you normally would on a typewriter (only you don't have to hit the carriage return at the end of each line). At any time, you can stop typing and give the computer commands to change the document, and then go back to typing again.

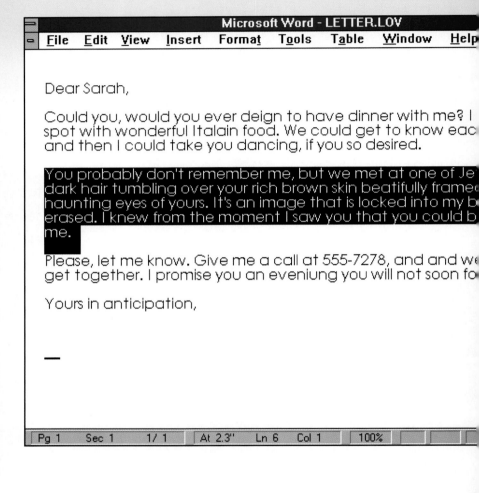

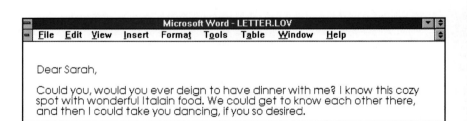

By saving the document on a disk, you can bring it back into the word processing program any time you want to change it, reuse it, or print it again!

FACTS

Word processing programs have a lot of powerful features beyond the basic ones needed for simple composing. They can, for example, handle automatic placement of footnotes. If you're writing a novel and decide to change the lead character's name from *Brad* to *Ernie*, you can have the program search for every instance of *Brad* and replace it with *Ernie*. You can change the margins or the tab stops, and the program will automatically reformat the entire document for you.

A lot of word processing programs are designed around people who use them all the time, and include every possible feature and command that anyone could ever want. These are often called **professional** word processing programs.

Because a professional program has so many commands, it can be hard for someone who doesn't use it often to find the command needed. For people like that, there are programs called **executive** word processing programs, which have only the small number of commands that most people really need.

The second paragraph would probably read better as the first paragraph. With word processing, you can issue commands to cut a specific block of text out of the document, and paste it in where you would rather have it.

Word processing programs have spelling dictionaries built-in. You will be offered a list of words that are close to what you typed, so that if it is a misspelling you don't have to guess the right spelling. (In this example, the spell checker also will catch the misspellings of Italian *and* evening. *The spell checker will even ask about the duplication of the word* and *in the last paragraph as a possible typing error.)*

When you're done making changes, and the document is in the form you want, just issue the command and it will come out perfect on the printer, the first time!

DESKTOP PUBLISHING

Desktop publishing is closely linked to word processing. While the main goal of a word processing program is to let you edit your text until your words are perfect, the main goal of a desktop publishing program is to let you change the way text (and pictures) fit onto the page until it looks perfect.

Desktop publishing programs (also called desktop publishers) are not designed to handle the *creation* of large amounts of text. You can put a few lines directly into the desktop publishing program, but for anything long, you will want to use your word processing program. The desktop publishing program will be able to work with the copy of your word processing text that you saved on disk, and use it as an element of the desktop publishing document.

Desktop publishing programs also let you use pictures that have been stored on disk. You can buy clip art (pre-drawn pictures for your computer), or you can use pictures that you created yourself with an art program (discussed later in this chapter), or even normal paper pictures that you put into your computer using a scanner (which is discussed in Chapter 14, "What Happens When You Use Your Scanner?").

Desktop publishing programs not only allow you to include pictures in your document, but will let you flow the text around the picture. Some only let you flow around the square edge of the picture, while some let you fit text very smoothly around jagged images.

THE CAPTAIN CO
FAN CLUB NEWSLET

Well, fans, the new season of The Captain Cookie Show starts next week, and reports out of Hollywood indicate that this will be the best one yet! If you're not tuned in on Saturday morning, you won't know what you're missing.

The first episode of the new season is MY CRUMBY FRIEND, during which Cap gets a new sidekick. Those of us who remember the last time the Crunchy Crusader got a sidekick know what a mistake that was. Luckily, they got rid of "Kid Cracker" after only three episodes, but those were three of the worst episodes in the entire run of the series! However, the producers promise us that the new sidekick, Snacky Sam, is nothing like K.C. While K.C. was constantly whining, never helping, and was held hostage in every single episode he was in, Snacky Sam is an industrious young cookie. Sure, Captain Cookie might have to save him from time to time, but then again, he'll have to save the Captain as well!

The seco
MUNCH
of our fa
dead in
the seve
Deadly
several
surpris
voice;
in all o
from
Repla
provi
mem
well
of In

Als
Mc
ev
are
th
Le
p

Now the bad news: Because of rising costs
rates by $2 per year. We will be giving you
however, and plan to make it a complete e
your renewal notice.

The desktop publisher allows you to use larger and fancier type styles, as well as putting text at angles and other fancy tricks.

FACTS

These days, word processing programs have features similar to desktop publishing programs, allowing you a great degree of control over typefaces, the flow of text through columns, and even putting pictures into your documents. As such, you might not really need a desktop publisher; a good word processing program may give you everything that you need.

If you do need a desktop publisher, consider carefully just what you need it for. Some desktop publishers are great for doing small jobs like short newsletters, invitations, etc. Other desktop publishers may not have as many nifty graphic tricks, but will automatically flow text across many pages.

Remember, just because a desktop publisher will give you the tools of a professional layout designer, that does not mean it will give you the talent. Many people start using a desktop publisher and find they need help producing attractive documents. There are plenty of books and classes to teach you how to get good, readable pages.

There also are templates available for the most popular desktop publishing programs. These are predesigned pages that you just add text to. Many programs come with some templates included.

(continued from page 1)
Myron, has become a father for the thir
Laura gave birth to little Tony Malone o
Murph says that the baby "sounds just l
referring to the western character he di
series Kartoon Kapers.
Meanwhile, L. Lois Wallace, who prov
Captain, has been appearing on broa
Loves. The show is planning a pa

The desktop publisher also makes it easy to flow text from page to page, allowing you to lay out a full magazine or book.

S MAN, THIS
he Deadly Donut, one
ure looked like he was
ce ("Donuts To You,"
st season), but The
back from the dead
this comes as no
e as a surprise is his
portrayed the character
pearances, has retired
r health reasons.
Pietrantonio, who has
Rasty Rusty and several
vil Squad in the past, as
voice on The Adventures

s season will be Doctor
ible Tucker Triplets, and
villainess, Jennifervor. There
s planned for Leroy Lizard,
use Kirk Quinn (who provided
gotten divorced from show
iller.

s, Murph Malone, who plays
r,
ge 3)

ave to raise subscription
r year for that money,
re details will be sent with

Adding lines, boxes, and shading can highlight text and make a nice looking page.

KEEPING RECORDS

We're surrounded by information that needs to be stored and maintained. At work, you might have customer lists, product lists, or order slips filling up file cabinets. At home, you're likely to have an address book, and maybe a list of CDs in your CD collection. Each is a set of units of information. Each unit (reflecting one customer, one product order, or one CD) is called a record.

You probably have these records in alphabetic order, so that it's easy to find the one you want quickly. But what happens when you need to find some of the records based on something besides name? What if you're planning a trip to New York, and need to find the addresses of all your friends who live there?

If you do it yourself, you have to check through every record on paper, looking for ones that match whatever you are looking for (your criteria). If you have a lot of records, this process can be simple but repetitive, boring, and cumbersome.

A database program can keep track of your sets of records, and can sort the records, find specific records, and create special lists of records far quicker than any person can.

Last name: JOSEPHSON   First name: CHARLES
Address: 809 MONTANA AVE
City: RIVERTON   State: NJ   ZIP: 08083
Phone: (609) 555 - 8229
Number of orders: 13   Last order date: 12/17/93
Amount outstanding: $700   Due since: 01/10/94
Salesman: BILL

08/29/93
Number of orders:
Amount outstanding: $35
Salesman: BILL

01/06/94
Amount outstanding: $1000
Salesman: TERRY

The program can select records based on whatever criteria you select. In this case, the computer is selecting based on calculated criteria: the "amount outstanding" is not 0.

Last name: JOSEPHSON First name: CHARLES
Address: 809 MONTANA AVE
City: RIVERTON   State: NJ   ZIP: 08083
Phone: (609) 555 - 8229
Number of orders: 13
Amount outstanding: $700   Last order date: 12/17/93
Salesman: BILL   Due since: 01/10/94

With a database program, you store a set of records called a database *(because it is a gathering, or "base," of information, or "data"). The database is just a computer file stored on disk, but it acts a lot like any organized filing system. For each set of records, you design a form which will hold all of the information that you need about each item. Whenever you add a new record to your set, the form comes up on the computer screen, and you enter all of the information using the keyboard. You also can bring up existing records and change them as needed.*

OVERDUE ACCOUNTS IN ORDER OF AMOUNT OWED			
Last Name	First Name	Phone	Amount Owed
Walters	Jeremiah	(312) 555-9871	$1000
Josephson	Charles	(609) 555-8229	$ 700
Gould	Angela	(212) 555-1201	$ 35

The program can print reports of whatever records you have selected, and sort them based on any of the information in those records. And remember that when it does this, it's not removing any records from your database, just copying information out of them—so you don't have to put anything back!

FACTS

Database programs come in a wide range of sophistication, from easy to use to extremely powerful but complex programs. The most advanced programs are actually programming languages designed specifically to handle database needs, and require someone with a good understanding of programming to use them effectively. If your needs are straightforward, a simple database program is usually sufficient.

If you need something very special—and don't feel comfortable programming it yourself—you can often get someone else to program it for you. Then you would use the program just created, which probably wouldn't be very flexible, but would be designed specifically to fit your needs. Be sure that you can get in touch with the programmer should something go wrong, or should your needs change.

A good database program can work hand-in-hand with a good word processing program to print out form letters. You use the database program to create a special computer file listing the people and addresses that you want to mail letters to. With a word processing feature called mail merge, you automatically put each of these names and addresses into a form letter, and print out each form letter.

DOING MATH

Since the computer turns everything into a number, it should come as no surprise that it is good for handling all sorts of mathematical problems. The main program that people use for doing math on a computer is a spreadsheet.

A spreadsheet does for calculations what a word processing programs does for words. You start with what is effectively a big empty page, and fill it up with all sorts of numbers and formulas. You tell the computer which numbers to add, to multiply, or to perform any other mathematical process on, and it will do it. You will quickly be able to see the numbers that you put in and the results that came out. You also can change any of the numbers, and the computer will automatically change the results to match. You can correct formulas, move numbers around, and copy them, just like you would with a word processing program.

The spreadsheet document is a grid, normally made up of numbered rows and lettered columns. Each intersection of a row and a column is called a cell. Each cell is referred to by the letter of the column and the number of the row that it is in; A3, C7, and G17 are all names of different cells.

...or a formula. The information each cell is actually typed in a line above the document display, but it then stored in the cell itself. At this point, the highlighted cell (B6) is going to store an equation which add together the values of the three cells above it (B3, B4, and B5).

...or a number, which will be used in your calculation...

Into each cell, you can put a label, words which will help you keep track of what is in the document...

2		MONDAY	
3	Jelly-filled		13
4	Sprinkles		9
5	Chocolate		27
6	TOTAL DONUTS		49
7			

While the computer stores *the equation entered into the cell, it* displays *the results of the equation.*

4	Sprinkles		9
5	Chocolate		27
6	TOTAL DONUTS		49
7	Price Per		0.35
8	TOTAL SALES		17.15
9			

This "total sales" cell holds another equation, multiplying the value of cell B6 by the value of cell B7. Since B6 is itself an equation cell, the result of that equation is being used.

2		MONDAY	
3	Jelly-filled		17
4	Sprinkles		9
5	Chocolate		27
6	TOTAL DONUTS		53
7	Price Per		0.35
8	TOTAL SALES		18.55

When the value in cell B3 is changed to 17, the value displayed in B6 is changed automatically, because it is partly based on cell B3. And because B6 changes, B8, which is based on B6, changes automatically as well!

FACTS

Spreadsheets can handle all sorts of formulas. In addition to simple mathematics, you can enter calculations that will compute averages, compound interest, advanced statistical calculations, and many other complex mathematical needs.

The spreadsheet program can not only print all or part of the document, but it also can create graphs based on the numbers in the spreadsheet document (or worksheet).

Modern spreadsheets have some database functions built in. These aren't as advanced as an advanced database program, or as easy to use as an easy-to-use database, but can prove quite useful, particularly when you need to perform advanced arithmetic functions on items in the database.

There are programs designed to help with advanced mathematics beyond arithmetic, such as complex algebra and calculus. These are great for those working on advanced engineering challenges, but are not particularly useful for more mundane needs.

PAINTING AND DRAWING

The computer, with all its technology, would seem to be an artist's nightmare. Yet, more and more people are doing artwork on computers. Computer art is actually a very attractive medium, because it is easy, precise, forgiving, and you don't have to wear a smock.

It's easy, because a computer drawing program is designed to allow you to fill in large areas with color, or take a small part of a picture and copy it all over the picture, all with just a couple of quick commands.

It's precise, because the computer is precise by its very nature. People complain that they cannot even draw a straight line, but with a computer, they don't have to. Just tell the computer where the line begins and ends, and the computer will draw it for you.

It's forgiving, because if you make a mistake, you can undo what you just did. And you can always save your drawing onto a disk, and then keep changing it on-screen. If you don't like the changes you made, you still have the version you liked on disk. Try doing that with a painting!

There are two main types of drawing programs: draw programs and paint programs.

Paint programs often leave rough edges—especially if you enlarge a painting.

In a paint program, your artwork is made up of a grid of little dots. You put colors down as sloppily or as precisely as your heart desires, even changing colors of individual dots. When you tell a paint program to draw a circle, it fills in all the dots within a roughly circular range with the color you chose. If you print a picture with a circle in it on a very sharp computer printer, what you get won't be a smooth circle, but a roughly circular shape of very sharp-edged squares.

FACTS

There are many programs that let you draw and design three-dimensional objects. You can't actually see them in 3-D on-screen, of course, but you can look at the objects from various angles.

Some of these 3-D programs are designed for computer aided designing (CAD). These are very useful in the engineering of machine parts, designing buildings, creating landscaping, and the like.

Other 3-D programs are designed to handle computer animation. Once you design a set of objects in 3-D, you can give commands to make them move around and even move the "camera" (point of view) around, and save the picture after each little piece of movement. It can take a long time for the computer to render each picture after each little move, but when the pictures are all stored and played back in sequence, the effect can be astonishing.

Draw programs create smooth edges that can be resized without getting any rough edges.

A draw program deals in very precise objects: lines, curves, circles, boxes, etc. It will handle a freehand squiggle by redefining it as a precise series of curves. While the computer has to translate all of these precise objects into a grid of dots in order to display them, it still stores them as precise objects. A circle is stored as "a circle this big centered at this location." That way, when you print out a picture with a circle in it, it is as sharp a circle as the printer can manage. Draw programs are very good for making charts, and for drafting.

TELECOMMUNICATIONS

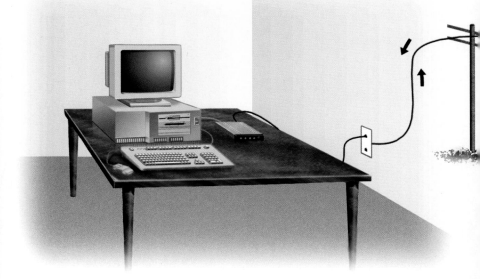

Using a modem, your computer can exchange messages with other computers over telephone lines.

There are all sorts of computers waiting for your call. Local bulletin board systems (or BBS's) are generally usable free of charge. The name "bulletin board system" is very descriptive of how people exchange messages there. People "post" messages that can be read by anyone, and other people enter messages in response. These messages are generally organized into categories, and old messages are taken off when room is needed for new ones. Most systems also have computer programs that you can download and keep. You also can send private mail (called electronic mail or e-mail) to other people who use the BBS.

In addition, there are international telecommunications services. Using services like CompuServe, America On-line, Prodigy, and GEnie, you can use your computer to access news, sports, weather, and stock information. You can even make airline and hotel reservations! All this wonderful stuff has a price, but it can be well worth it.

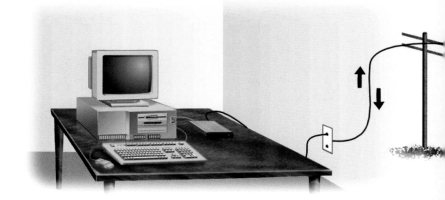

With an international service, you connect to a local phone number, where a bank of modems is collecting information from a large number of computers dialing in, and forwarding it to the central computer over a special high-speed line. Thousands of people can be connected to the on-line service at once. While they are on-line, they can get information and also be involved in immediate, typed conversations with large groups of other users who are on the system at the same time.

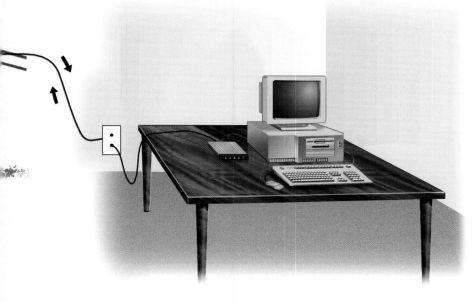

Using a telecommunications program, you tell your computer to dial the telephone number of the BBS. The modem and the computer of the BBS answer the phone. From then until you hang up, every keystroke is sent down the phone line to the other computer, and the computer sends information back to be displayed on-screen. Effectively, your computer is just acting as a window to allow you to use a program running on the BBS.

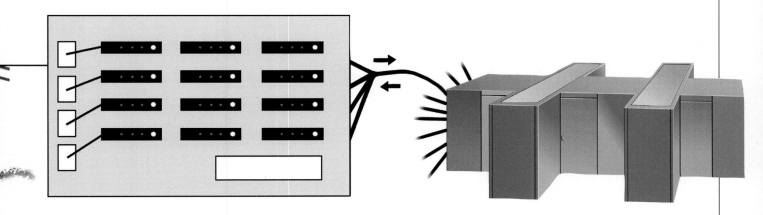

With a computer network like Internet, instead of dialing directly into a distant computer, messages get sent from computer to computer like a bucket brigade, until it reaches the target computer. Internet has a vast web of machines, supported mostly by colleges, and provides hundreds of thousands of people with private mail and public conversations.

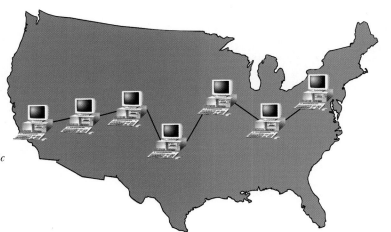

GAMES

Thinking of games as too frivolous and unimportant for a serious discussion of computers would be easy—and wrong. Game playing is one of the most common uses of personal computers, and also has been a key driving force behind the advancement and the popularization of computers.

Just as games have been important to computers, computers also have been important to games. Computers enhance traditional games by allowing people to play without having to find a human partner. With the right computer program, a person can play backgammon or dominos while alone. You can play chess against a challenger as powerful or inept as you want. You can even play roulette, blackjack, and craps without heading to Atlantic City, although fortunately the computer is not set up to collect all your money and then loan you more at high interest rates.

But more impressive is the broad array of games that are unlike anything that could be done before the computer.

Adventure games are really more like long compli-cated puzzles than games. The player has a limited set of commands that he or she uses to control a character in a fictional, fantasy world, trying to get him or her past various obstacles.

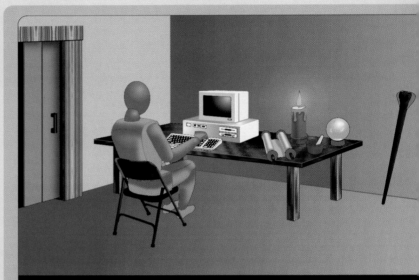

You find yourself in room with two exits, to the nor
There is a personal computer on a desk with a chair.
Deathdealer?

> Sit down

You are now seated at the computer.

> Type "Help"

FACTS

Many games attempt to simulate real-world situations, although the levels of reality that they achieve (or even strive for) vary greatly.

Sports simulations put you in control of players or even entire teams in games both real and fanciful. These keep the strategic aspects of traditional sports, while replacing sheer physical exertion with simple manual dexterity—finally, a way to be involved in sports without actually getting any exercise! (Similarly, war simulations allow people to control armies and act as generals, while avoiding the death and dismemberment that often accompany such a career.)

Flight simulators simulate the experience of being a pilot. Some of these strive for a great deal of realism, allowing a full set of controls and re-creating a range of weather and terrain conditions. These can be useful tools for learning to fly a real plane. Others turn flying into a combat action game, sending players anywhere from a World War I dogfight to a mission to blow up the sinister space station of the evil Znedsaurians.

Arcade games bring the endless action and finger-pounding excitement of the video arcade into your otherwise quiet home (or office—you can often catch coworkers saving the world from space aliens or rescuing a stranded prince when they should be finishing the quarterly report). Joystick controllers are available for playing these games.

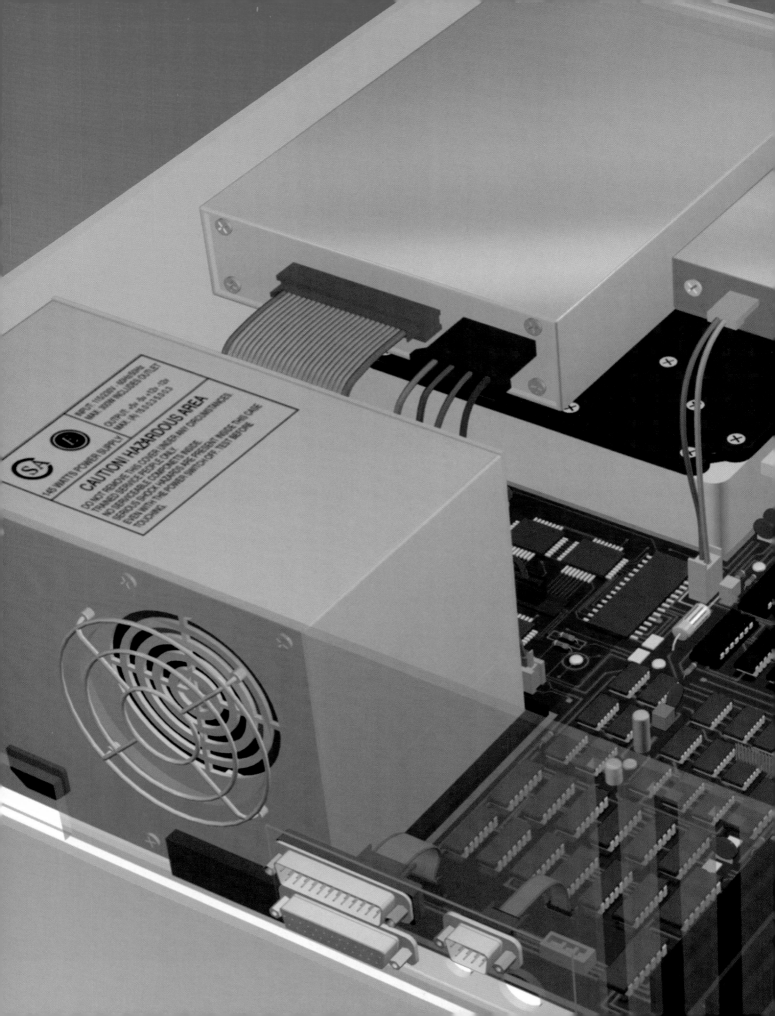

CAUTION HAZARDOUS AREA

DO NOT REMOVE THIS COVER UNDER ANY CIRCUMSTANCES
TRAINED SERVICE PEOPLE ONLY
NO SERVICEABLE COMPONENTS INSIDE
SERIOUS SHOCK HAZARDS ARE PRESENT INSIDE THIS CASE
EVEN WITH THE POWER SWITCH OFF. TEST BEFORE
TOUCHING

145 WATTS POWER SUPPLY

INPUT 110/220V 60/50Hz
MAX 300W INCLUDES OUTLET

OUTPUT +5v 9v +12v -12v
MAX IA 18.0/2.0/0.3

CHAPTER

3

BASIC
COMPUTER ANATOMY

BASIC COMPUTER ANATOMY

Desktop PCs are made from standardized, interchangeable parts, so the basics do not vary much from machine to machine. The cabinets may be shaped somewhat differently, or the disk drives may be arranged differently, but PCs are, in general, very much alike.

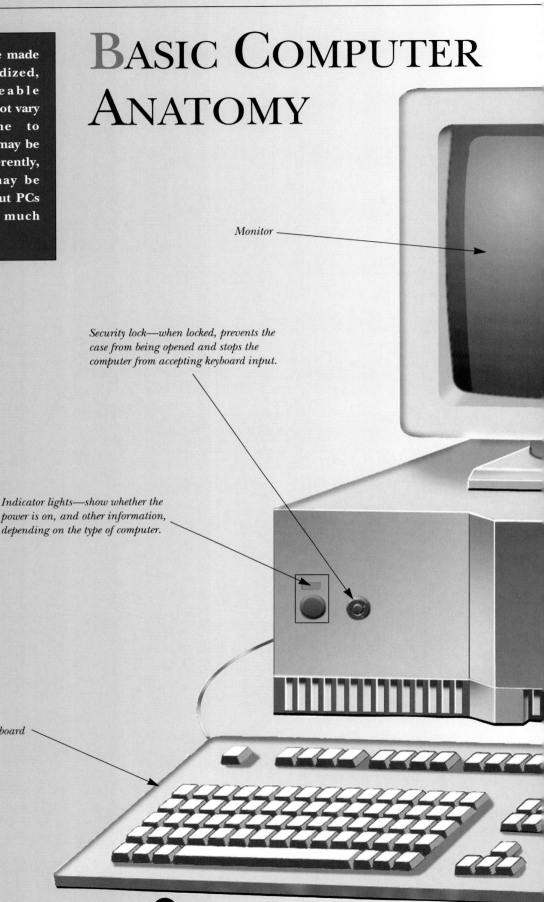

Monitor

Security lock—when locked, prevents the case from being opened and stops the computer from accepting keyboard input.

Indicator lights—show whether the power is on, and other information, depending on the type of computer.

Keyboard

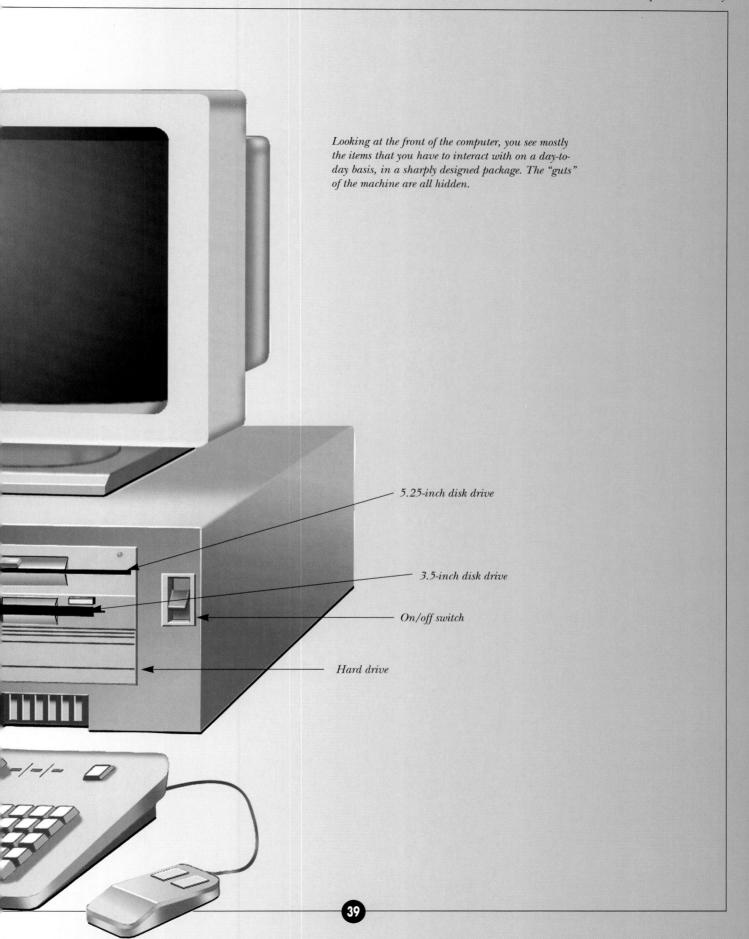

Looking at the front of the computer, you see mostly the items that you have to interact with on a day-to-day basis, in a sharply designed package. The "guts" of the machine are all hidden.

5.25-inch disk drive

3.5-inch disk drive

On/off switch

Hard drive

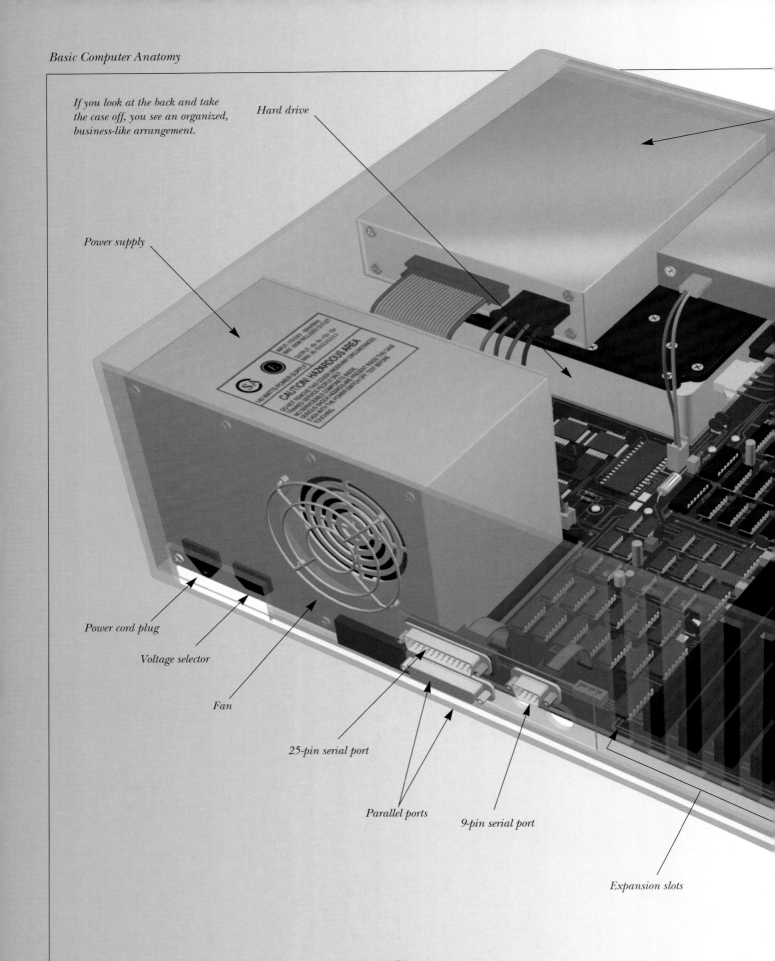

*If you look at the back and take
the case off, you see an organized,
business-like arrangement.*

Hard drive

Power supply

Power cord plug

Voltage selector

Fan

25-pin serial port

Parallel ports

9-pin serial port

Expansion slots

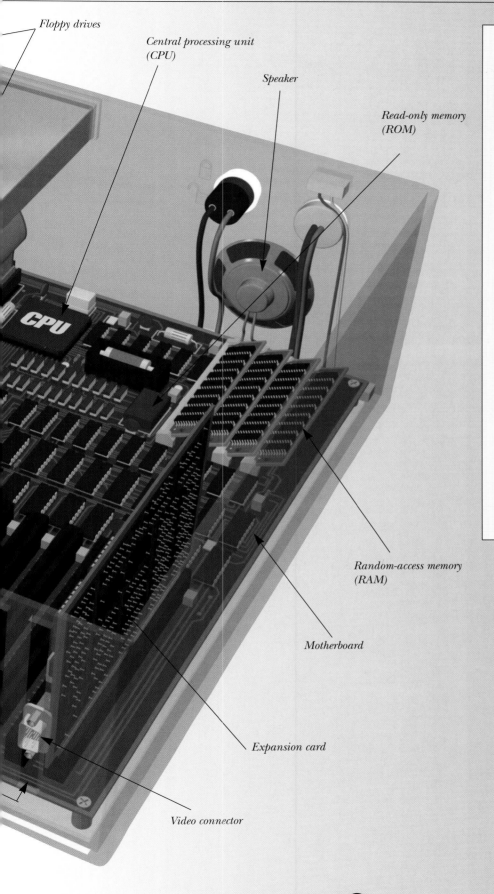

Floppy drives

Central processing unit
(CPU)

Speaker

Read-only memory
(ROM)

Random-access memory
(RAM)

Motherboard

Expansion card

Video connector

FACTS

This figure shows a desktop computer. There are other types of personal computers which are organized differently, but the basic components are the same.

Tower computer configurations are popular; these are a lot like this design only turned sideways, with the disk drives toward the top. Tower units are nice because you can put them next to or under your desk, with just the keyboard and monitor actually on the desk, taking up much less desk space. (The amount of surface space that a computer takes up is called the footprint.)

Laptop computers have similar components, only more compact, as weight and space are more important considerations than expandability.

In Chapter 1, "What Is a Computer?," you saw that the computer keeps information and performs calculations using a lot of little switches. The computer doesn't use mechanical switches like light switches, but the concept is very much the same.

TRANSISTOR SWITCHES

Electricity flows from where there is a negative charge to where there is a positive charge, but only when there is a path of something like metal to carry it. Metal carries electricity well, so it is considered a *conductor*.

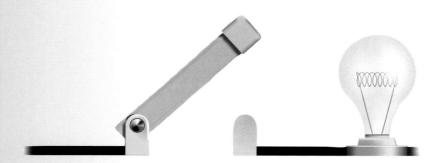

Open a switch and you interrupt the metal path with air. Air does not carry electricity (which means it's an *insulator*), so the electricity no longer has a path to flow through.

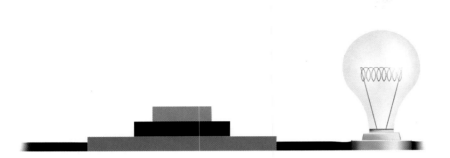

A transistor is a special arrangement of materials. There's a conductor layer, a layer of insulating material, and then a layer of a very special insulator on the bottom. Because it's an insulator, electricity won't flow through it.

FACTS

Computer transistors are so small that a million of them fit per square inch of a flat wafer called a chip. (The chip is generally enclosed in a black casing with tiny metal rods to attach it to other components. The whole little package also is referred to as a chip.) They aren't each placed on the chip and then soldered together; they're basically painted on using an extremely fine stencil.

The special material used to make the transistors is a mixture of chemicals based on the element silicon, a light metal which is a major component of sand. That's why you sometimes hear computer chips called "silicon chips" (the area of California where all the computer companies are located is called "Silicon Valley").

What makes that last layer special is that when there is a certain electrical charge to the first layer, the insulator turns into a conductor! Electricity then flows through the material, just like when you turn a switch on. Two kinds of transistors are used: one where the switch turns on only if you apply a positive electrical charge to the top layer, and one that turns on only with a negative charge.

(+)

The motherboard (also known as the system board) is where all the computer's built-in electronics reside. Everything else—peripherals like the disk drives, and additional boards like modems or video adapters—are attached to the motherboard, and they exchange information with it. That's why it's called a "mother"—the other boards and components are its children.

The motherboard has metallic circuits printed onto it, and via this circuitry the chips and components on the board exchange the electronic impulses that carry information.

THE MOTHERBOARD

RAM slots

CPU

Clock chip; runs off of a battery, so that the date and time information is constantly maintained.

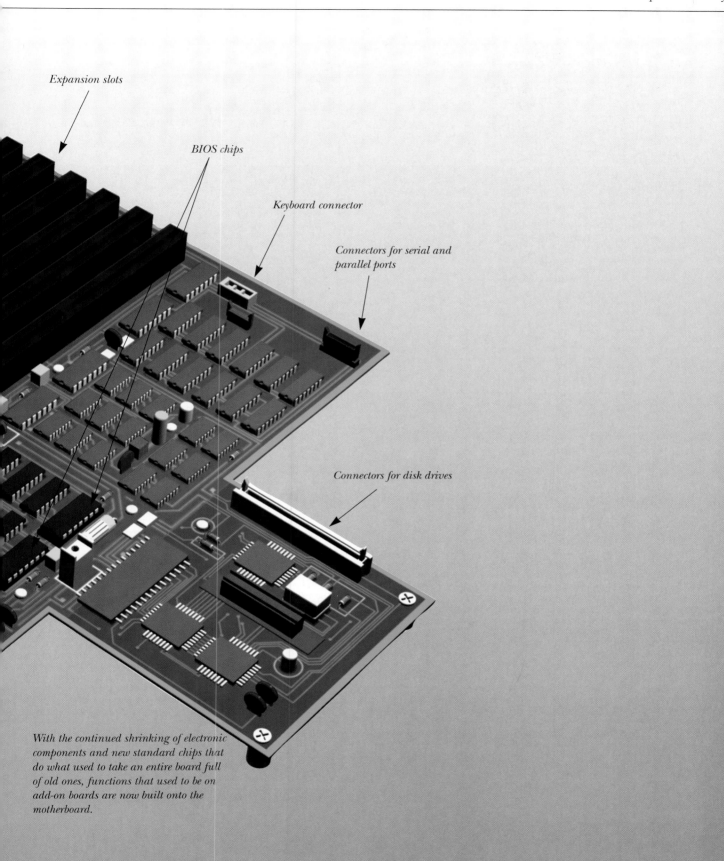

Expansion slots

BIOS chips

Keyboard connector

Connectors for serial and parallel ports

Connectors for disk drives

With the continued shrinking of electronic components and new standard chips that do what used to take an entire board full of old ones, functions that used to be on add-on boards are now built onto the motherboard.

THE CENTRAL PROCESSING UNIT

The central processing unit, also called the CPU or processor, is the brain of the machine. This simple-looking chip is what does the processing. The rest of the computer is designed to service the CPU, to interface with the user, and to store and retrieve information. It's the CPU that understands the commands, runs the programs, and makes the whole thing work.

PCs are built around a family of processor chips designed by Intel, starting with the 8088. Every few years, there is a major leap to the next generation of processors: the 8086 came next, followed by the 80286 and then the 80386 (the oldest processor that PCs are still built around), then the 486, and now the Pentium. Each of these chips is more powerful than the previous one, able to handle a wider array of commands, and deal with more data, more quickly, while still able to run the software designed for the previous generation. But there is some question as to whether that is still the way that things will continue to advance, as you will see.

There are about three million transistors inside the Pentium chip. This diagram shows a simplified version of the logical flow within the processor.

8K BYTE DATA CACHE

ADDRESS AND BUS HANDLERS

OUT TO THE BUS (RAM, I/O, ETC.)

The address and bus handlers deal with the world outside the chip, getting information in from the RAM and input/ output devices and sending information to them.

Using complex logic, the Pentium chip constantly guesses what RAM locations the command unit will next need to read, and gets that information ahead of time. Commands and data are stored in separate caches. This doesn't work 100% of the time, but it works often enough and speeds things up enough (reading from the caches is faster than reading from memory) that it is worthwhile. When a command writes data into memory, the Pentium has to see if it has cached the information for that memory location and, if so, change that value in the cache as well.

FACTS

Other manufacturers are placing their bets on future processors with a very different philosophy: Reduced Instruction Set Computing (RISC). Instead of being designed to handle powerful commands like traditional Complex Instruction Set Computing (CISC), **RISC** processors handle a very limited, simple, straightforward set of commands, but do them very fast. The idea is that if you take enough baby steps fast enough, you will go faster than someone who takes much longer but slower strides.

A lot of programs have been designed around existing generations of CISC processors. RISC processors won't directly understand the old complex instructions. To run old programs, the RISC processors will run an emulator program that will take each complex instruction and translate it into a number of simpler instructions, and then execute the simpler instructions.

State-of-the-art RISC and CISC processors both use around two to three million transistors. This is about 100 times as many transistors as were in the 8088 chip that ran the original IBM PC.

Experts expect processors with around 100 million transistors by the turn of the century.

The Pentium processor is so complex that it is basically a complete little computer within itself, with its own RAM and internal input/output (I/O) system. The command unit at its core actually executes the command. The commands that it executes either tell it to change the data stored in the special registers within it, or to pass information to another part of the CPU chip.

The registers are memory storage locations that the command processor interacts with directly. Some hold address information, such as where in RAM the next command is to come from.

The command unit passes requests for trigonometric or logarithmic mathematical functions to the floating point unit (FPU). The FPU handles such things much faster than the system could without it. Some earlier chips in this family did not contain an FPU, so users who did a lot of scientific or graphic work purchased a chip designed specifically to provide that function.

The Instruction Prefetch anticipates which command is next. In the case of certain very simple commands, the Pentium can actually execute two commands at once.

FETCH
COMMAND UNIT
REGISTERS
FLOATING POINT UNIT

Random-access memory, or RAM, is high-speed, short-term memory where the computer stores the information it is working with. This includes the program or programs that the computer is running, as well as any data that those programs are handling. This memory is inside special computer chips.

Each byte of information is stored in RAM at a location with a specific address number. The "random" refers to the fact that the computer can move from any address in memory with equal speed. This is in contrast to mechanical storage devices, like hard disk drives, that take longer to access data stored in addresses that are further away from the current address.

Memory works in units of bytes, each of which is eight bits. When we talk about amount of memory, we frequently talk in kilobytes. The prefix "kilo-" actually means "thousand," but a kilobyte of memory is 1,024 bytes. (1,024 is two to the tenth power, one of those powers of two which the computer finds easy to deal with.) "Kilobytes" is frequently abbreviated as KB or K.

Larger amounts of memory are measured in megabytes; "mega-" means "million," but a megabyte is actually 1,048,576 bytes (two to the 20th power). A megabyte is often just referred to as a meg, or MB.

RANDOM-ACCESS MEMORY

RAM chips are used in groups of nine, each holding the same number of bits (measured in kilobits or megabits). RAM is usually sold and installed already attached to a standard add-in board, called a Single In-line Memory Module, or SIMM.

Each byte is stored over eight chips, each of the chips holding one bit of every byte. When a byte is requested, each of the chips only has to put out one bit.

ADDRESS CONVERTER

Inside the RAM chip is a gridwork of transistor logic. Each bit stored has its own little circuitry. The address decoder takes the binary-coded memory address in and uses it to find the specific circuit that stores that bit.

Because RAM is electronic, when the power is turned off all of the stored data disappears.

SIMMs slide into a special angled socket, either on the motherboard or on an add-in memory board. Older machines frequently use socketed memory, where you have to put each chip separately into sockets.

FACTS

As chip prices have fallen and programs have gotten bigger and more memory-hungry, the amount of RAM in a PC has grown substantially. The earliest IBM PCs shipped with 16K of RAM. Few PCs today ship with less than two megabytes, more than 100 times as much.

RAM chips don't put information out instantly, although it is remarkably fast. Chip speed is measured in how long it takes to access a requested bit of information, and that speed is measured in nanoseconds, billionths of a second. Most memory sold these days falls into the 50 to 100 nanosecond range. It is important to use memory that is at least as fast as the system is designed for. It won't help you to put in faster chips but slower ones can cause problems.

The ninth chip holds the parity bit. For each byte stored, the system adds the bits together. The parity bit says whether the result is odd or even. Whenever a byte is retrieved, its bits are added again and the result is checked against the stored parity bit. When something goes wrong with one of the memory chips and it returns a wrong value, this system detects it instantly.

READ-ONLY MEMORY

Read-only memory (ROM) chips store programs permanently in a form that the CPU can easily read. It's read-only because the CPU can't write information into the ROM, it can only read information out of it. The information is placed into the ROM before the ROM is installed in the PC.

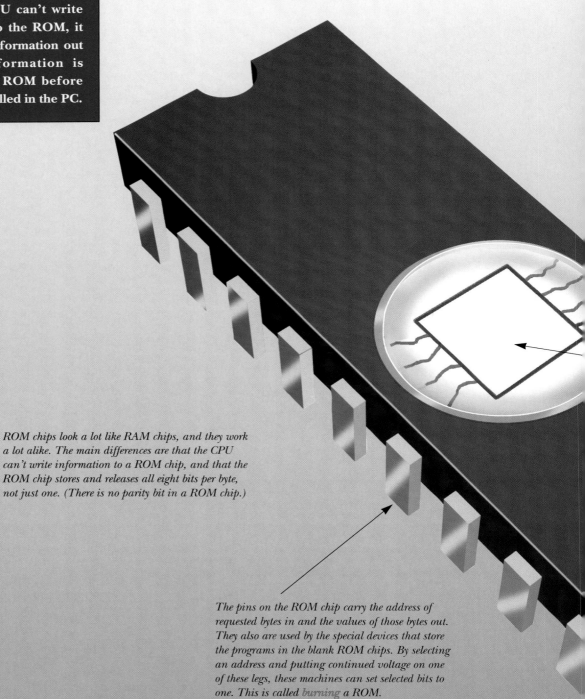

ROM chips look a lot like RAM chips, and they work a lot alike. The main differences are that the CPU can't write information to a ROM chip, and that the ROM chip stores and releases all eight bits per byte, not just one. (There is no parity bit in a ROM chip.)

The pins on the ROM chip carry the address of requested bytes in and the values of those bytes out. They also are used by the special devices that store the programs in the blank ROM chips. By selecting an address and putting continued voltage on one of these legs, these machines can set selected bits to one. This is called *burning* a ROM.

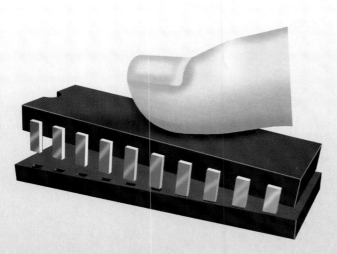

ROM chips are generally put into sockets on the motherboard, so that if there are any problems with the program on the chip, they can be removed and replaced.

Most ROM chips can have their memory cleared by ultraviolet radiation. Passing through the little window on the chip, it sets all of the bits to 0.

THE SYSTEM BUS

The system bus is the circuitry that the add-on cards and the peripherals use to communicate with the processor, the RAM, and each other. This is most visible at the sockets where the expansion cards can connect to the bus.

The availability of these standard expansion slots has helped PC-style computers to thrive. Because it's so easy to manufacturer and install expansion boards to supplement the PC's function, the PCs have proved very flexible for a broad array of uses, from controlling model trains to analyzing medical test results.

No board needs to access all of the lines on the bus, so they only provide contacts to the lines that they need. The contacts that take the power are on the opposite side of the card from the leads that carry data and addresses, to keep the power lines from causing interference.

The original PC expansion slots had 62 contacts, 31 on each side. Each contact connects to a circuit line with a special purpose. Eight carried data, one bit per line. Twenty lines carried memory address information, also one bit each (which made up to one megabyte of RAM addressable). Other lines carried electricity to power the boards. The rest served a variety of special purposes.

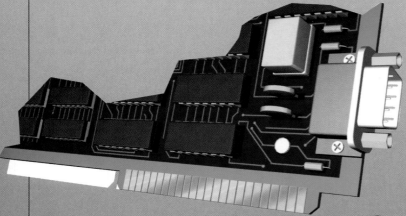

IBM came up with an even more powerful bus design, Micro-Channel Architecture, or MCA. This has a 116-contact version, which carries 16 bits of data at a time, and a 186-contact version, carrying 32 bits. This design provides a lot of advanced features that the ISA doesn't, but you can't plug cards designed for the ISA into it. IBM continues to make PCs with MCA buses, but they make up only a small portion of the PCs sold.

FACTS

On older PCs, the processor communicates with RAM over the system bus. However, as processors got faster and faster, the limited speed of the system bus couldn't keep up, so the memory was moved to the system board. The local bus was created just for the processor and the RAM to pass information back and forth.

Now, faster hard drives and video cards hook into the local bus rather than the system bus for their communications with the processor and the RAM. This gives them the faster access that they need, while the ISA bus is fine for modems, joystick adapters, sound cards, and other cards that don't need the speed of the local bus.

When more powerful buses became necessary, a second connector was added. These two connector buses are called Industry Standard Architecture (or ISA) buses. Cards using the second connector have access to 36 more circuit lines. Eight of these carry additional data, upping the amount of data that can flow at once to 16 bits. Four more lines were added to the addresses, letting the board access up to 16 megabytes of memory.

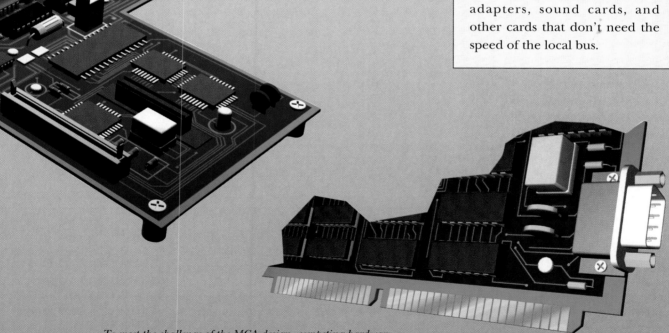

To meet the challenge of the MCA design, competing hardware manufacturers got together and came up with Extended Industry Standard Architecture, or EISA. This bus has capabilities similar to the MCA design, with one significant addition: ISA boards could fit into an EISA expansion slot. These are still available but have not gained much popularity.

DISK DRIVES

The disk drives store large amounts of information for long-term usage. While RAM is good for immediate, temporary high-speed storage, it loses its information when you turn off the machine, plus you only have a limited amount of storage.

Disk drives store information magnetically. That way it stays around even after you turn off the machine.

Hard disks store large amounts of information, often hundreds of megabytes. Most users keep all of the programs and data that they work with on the hard disk.

Floppy disks are designed to be inserted into and removed from floppy disk drives that are built into the machine. Each disk only stores about 1/3 to three megabytes, depending on the type of disk and drive. Floppy disks come in two sizes (3.5-inches wide and 5.25-inches wide).

Early PCs often had only floppy drives. However, the programs got bigger and bigger, until it became impossible to run them off of floppies. Luckily, the price of hard-drives had plummeted even as they were able to store more and more.

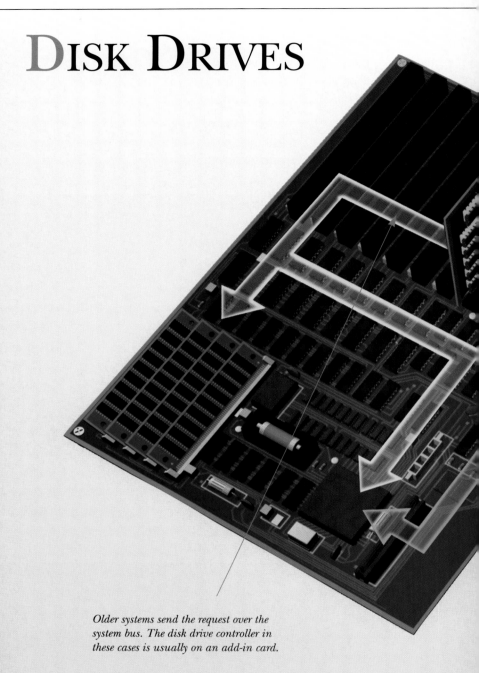

Older systems send the request over the system bus. The disk drive controller in these cases is usually on an add-in card.

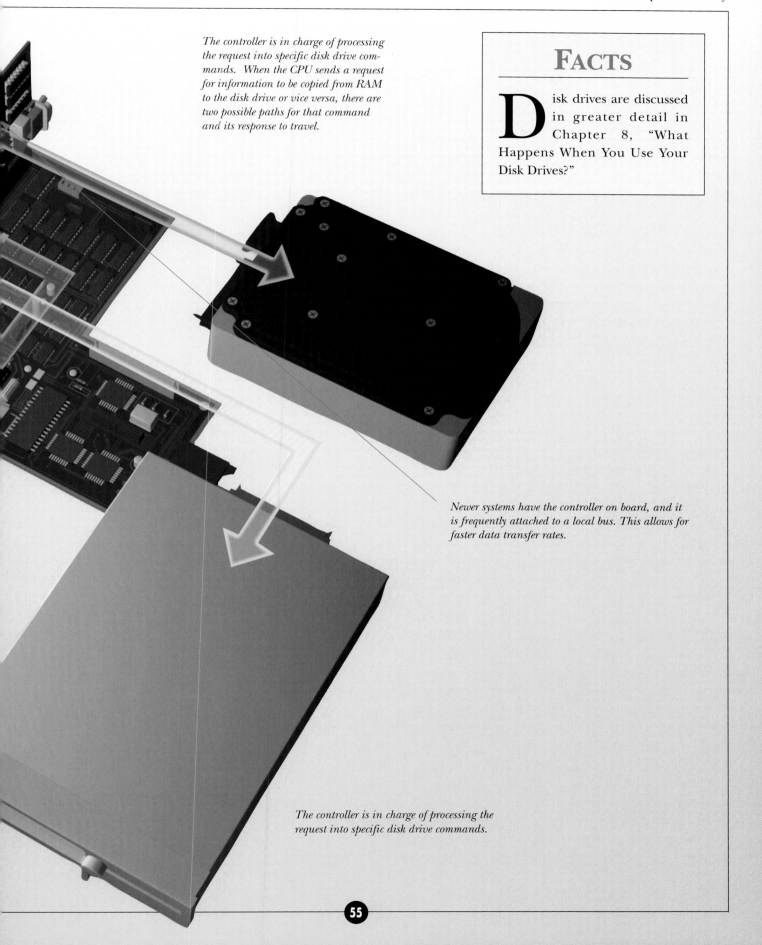

The controller is in charge of processing the request into specific disk drive commands. When the CPU sends a request for information to be copied from RAM to the disk drive or vice versa, there are two possible paths for that command and its response to travel.

FACTS

D isk drives are discussed in greater detail in Chapter 8, "What Happens When You Use Your Disk Drives?"

Newer systems have the controller on board, and it is frequently attached to a local bus. This allows for faster data transfer rates.

The controller is in charge of processing the request into specific disk drive commands.

I/O DEVICES

The PC has a number of ways to receive and transmit information to the outside world. These are referred to as I/O devices. (I/O is short for input/output.)

The keyboard and some other I/O devices have connections built into the PC specifically for them. Others (like scanners, printers, external modems, and some types of computer mouse) take advantage of general-purpose connectors called serial ports and parallel ports.

The serial ports, parallel ports, and keyboards all talk via the system bus. Because they aren't used for ultra-high-speed devices, there is no need to hook them up to the local bus.

Some mice connect to serial ports, and some have their own connections to the system bus.

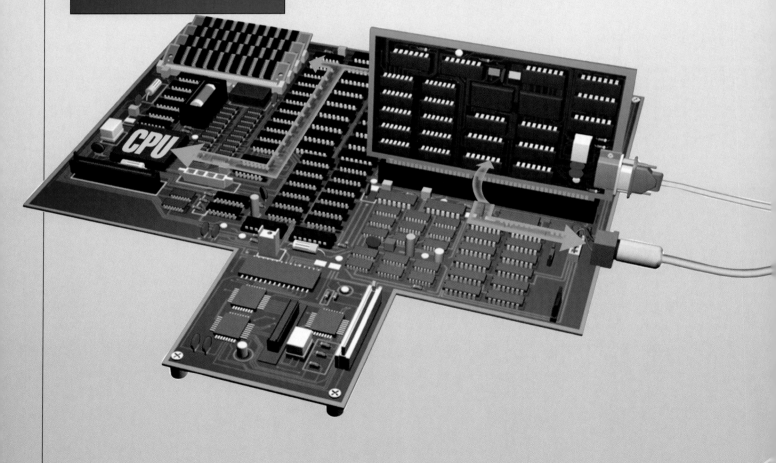

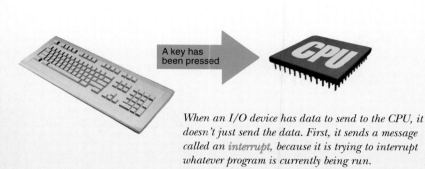

A key has been pressed

When an I/O device has data to send to the CPU, it doesn't just send the data. First, it sends a message called an interrupt, *because it is trying to interrupt whatever program is currently being run.*

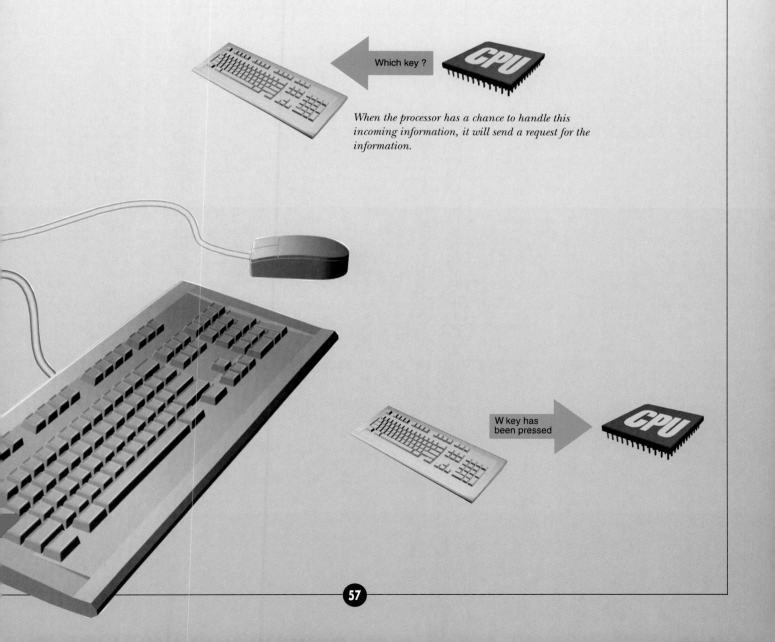

Which key ?

When the processor has a chance to handle this incoming information, it will send a request for the information.

W key has been pressed

THE VIDEO DISPLAY

The monitor or video display unit (VDU) is the television-like screen that the computer uses to show information to the user.

The earliest PCs could only display text and certain fixed graphics items that took up the full space of a single character. These were displayed in bright green against a greenish black background, in a system that seemed almost designed to strain your eyes.

The modern PC, however, displays high resolution graphics information in full, gorgeous color.

FACTS

The VDU and graphic adapter are covered in-depth in Chapter 10, "What Happens When You Use Your Monitor?"

The graphic adapter takes the screen information from RAM and turns it into a video signal that the VDU can display.

Traditionally, graphic adapters have used the system bus to get information from RAM. The latest high-speed graphic adapters tap into a local bus. While the graphic adapter still gets only relatively short, simple commands from the CPU, the increasing resolution and range of colors that the displays support mean a skyrocketing amount of information that must be accessed from the RAM. Local bus access speeds that up greatly.

POWER SYSTEM

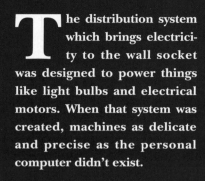

The distribution system which brings electricity to the wall socket was designed to power things like light bulbs and electrical motors. When that system was created, machines as delicate and precise as the personal computer didn't exist.

As such, the computer has a system set up to protect itself from electrical problems, as well as to process the electricity into a palatable form.

Surge protector/multi-socket adapter

The on/off switch is generally either on the right side of the PC (near the power supply), or on the front for convenient access.

*A **surge protector** isn't part of the computer itself, but an absolutely essential accessory. Not only does it multiply the number of electrical sockets available, but it also protects the system from uneven voltage. Lightning storms and powerful appliances can cause voltage surges and spikes that can ruin an unprotected computer.*

Many come with a phone line protector, to keep lightning surges from frying your modem and, through that, your computer.

The power supply takes the AC power (alternating current, switching direction roughly 60 times per second) that comes out of the wall, and turns it into DC power (direct current, going in a constant direction). The power supply puts out five-volt and 12-volt power for the various components inside.

FACTS

E ven with a surge protector, it is a good idea to turn off your computer and unplug it during electrical storms. A close and powerful lightning strike can move through a power supply and into the computer before the surge protector can cut the line.

Never open up the power supply. Even when the computer is unplugged, the power supply can hold voltage and give a dangerous shock. Handling the insides of power supplies should be left to those trained for it.

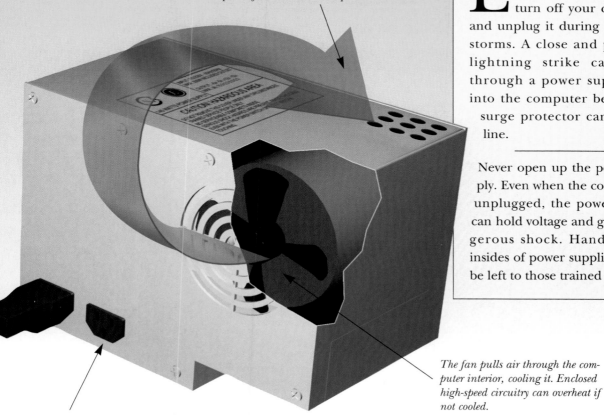

The fan pulls air through the computer interior, cooling it. Enclosed high-speed circuitry can overheat if not cooled.

A pass-through socket is provided on the back of the computer, where you can plug in the monitor. That way, if you leave the monitor switched on, it will turn on and off when you turn your computer on and off. Some monitors need more power than this socket provides.

An Uninterruptable Power Supply (or UPS) is essentially a large battery that stores energy. When you have a blackout or blown fuse, the UPS continues powering the computer system without a hiccup. More expensive models handle an extended outage for computers that have to stay on no matter what; cheaper models allow you several minutes to save your file and shut down your computer gracefully.

4

WHAT HAPPENS WHEN YOU TURN ON YOUR COMPUTER?

The Computer Checks Itself

The Basic Input/Output System

Finding the Operating System

The Operating System Adapts to You

When you first awake in the morning, you aren't immediately ready to do anything useful. First, you have to blink your eyes a bit and stretch your limbs to make sure everything's working.

Similarly, when the computer is first turned on, it's not ready to help you with your work. First, it has to blink its eyes and stretch its limbs to make certain everything is working.

WHAT HAPPENS WHEN YOU TURN ON YOUR COMPUTER?

1 *First, the system checks out the RAM and other parts, to make sure they work.*

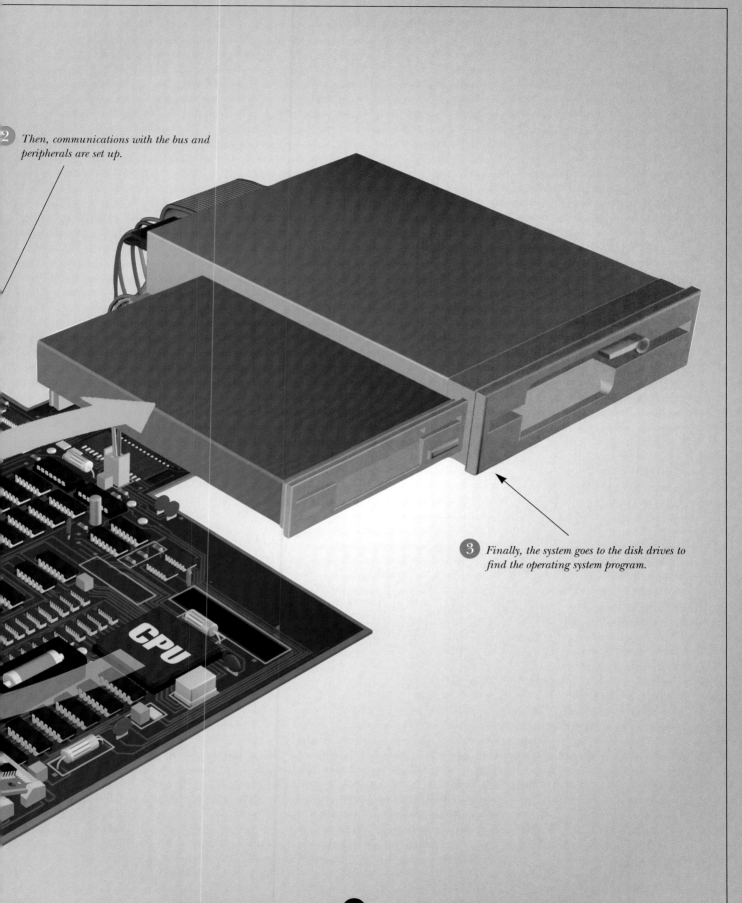

2 *Then, communications with the bus and peripherals are set up.*

3 *Finally, the system goes to the disk drives to find the operating system program.*

CPU

THE COMPUTER CHECKS ITSELF

The first thing the computer does when it is turned on is to check some of its most basic functions, to make sure that everything works properly. It does this by running a program stored in ROM, the Power On Self Test, or POST.

The CPU sends signals to check on the computer's different components. Most components respond by returning their own signals that state if they are okay or not okay. Other components are not expected to respond—the computer just needs to know if they are present.

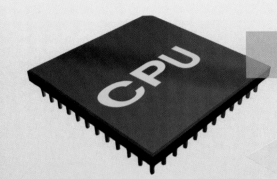

ARE YOU OKAY ?

I'M FIN[E]

OR

SOMETHING WRONG

OR

NO RESPONSE NON-VITAL PE[

SYSTEM **BEEPS** AND STOPS TESTING

This system runs a program, asking various devices to check themselves. Some non-vital devices may not need to respond. If the device is vital, and doesn't respond, the CPU will cause the system to beep.

FACTS

When you restart the computer by holding down the Ctrl, Alt, and Del keys simultaneously, the system skips over the POST. This startup procedure is called a warm boot.

In contrast, performing a cold boot causes your system to repeat all of the POST tests by fooling your computer into thinking it had been turned off and back on again. You can perform a cold boot by pressing the reset button on your PC. If you don't have a reset button, turn the computer off and back on.

The POST spends most of its time testing the system memory. The more memory you have, the longer the POST takes.

The POST program has a special test for RAM, which involves storing information in RAM, and then checking that it was stored correctly.

FOR
LS)

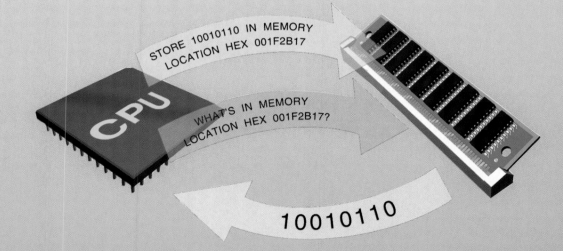

STORE 10010110 IN MEMORY LOCATION HEX 001F2B17

WHAT'S IN MEMORY LOCATION HEX 001F2B17?

10010110

THE BASIC INPUT/OUTPUT SYSTEM

The processor does not inherently know how to deal with keyboards, disk drives, and other peripherals. The Basic Input/Output System (BIOS) is a program that takes care of the most basic level of communication between the processor and the peripherals.

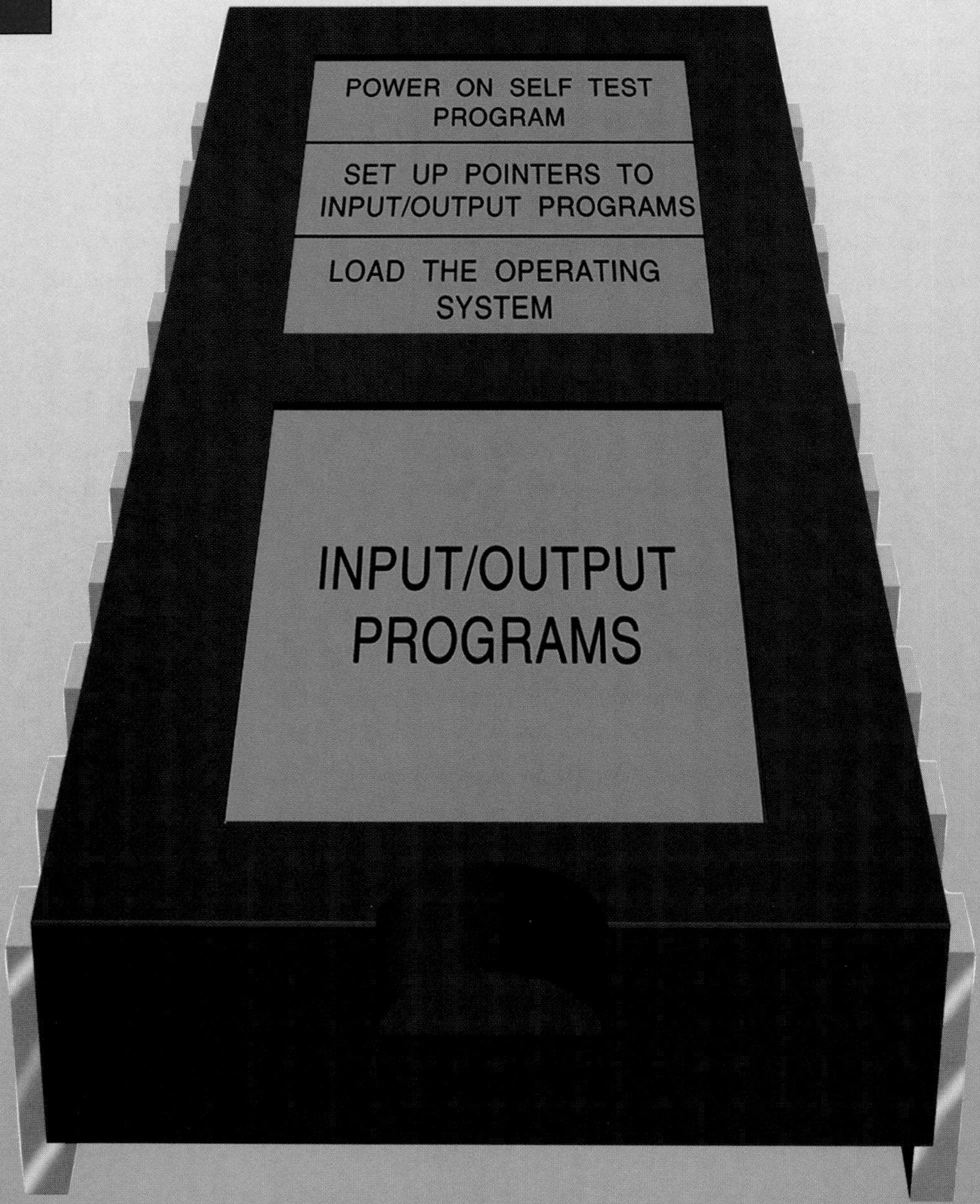

POWER ON SELF TEST PROGRAM

SET UP POINTERS TO INPUT/OUTPUT PROGRAMS

LOAD THE OPERATING SYSTEM

INPUT/OUTPUT PROGRAMS

The BIOS ROM programs can be divided into two parts. The first part is all of the startup procedures. The second part consists of programs that are called later to handle input and output.

FACTS

Because the map of the interrupt programs is in RAM, other programs can change it if they need to deal with the I/O devices in non-standard ways.

Depending on your system, your startup routines and BIOS may all be stored on one ROM chip, or may be spread out over several.

The CPU has a special register telling it where to find the map that shows where special programs to handle the input are stored. The startup procedure sets that special register to an area of RAM, and then has the map in RAM point back to programs stored in ROM.

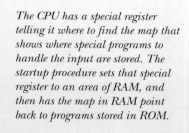

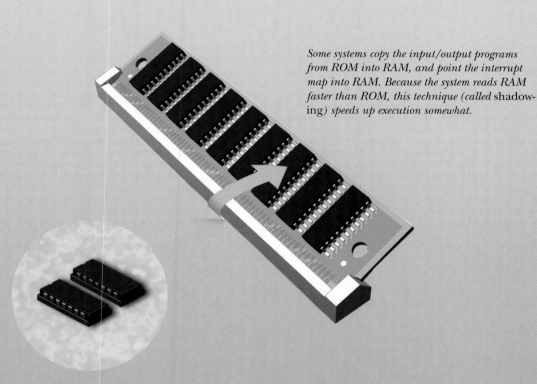

Some systems copy the input/output programs from ROM into RAM, and point the interrupt map into RAM. Because the system reads RAM faster than ROM, this technique (called shadowing*) speeds up execution somewhat.*

FINDING THE OPERATING SYSTEM

Once the interrupt system has been set up, the last part of the initialization program in the BIOS tries to load the operating system, the program that lets your computer know how to find and load other programs. Before the operating system can be loaded, though, it has to be found.

Computers with hard drives use this system, checking the floppy disk, and then the hard disk for an operating system.

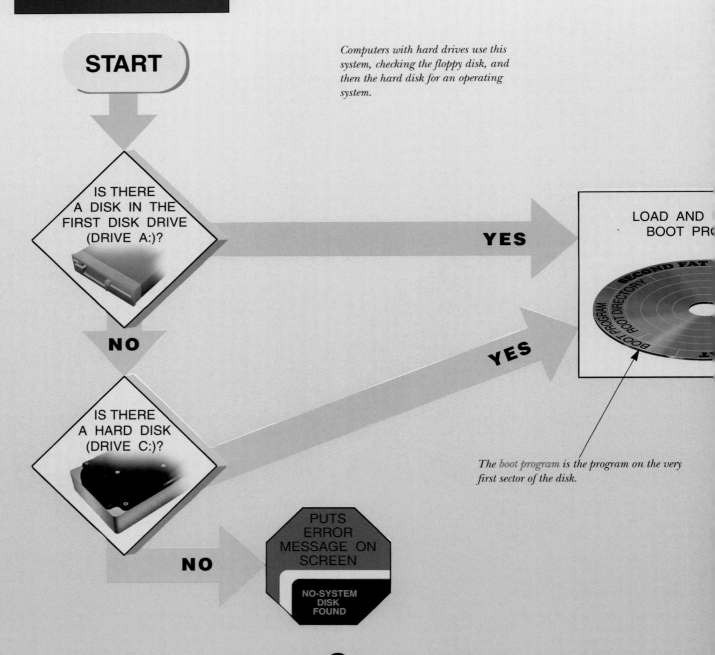

START

IS THERE A DISK IN THE FIRST DISK DRIVE (DRIVE A:)?

YES

LOAD AND BOOT PRO...

NO

YES

IS THERE A HARD DISK (DRIVE C:)?

The boot program is the program on the very first sector of the disk.

NO

PUTS ERROR MESSAGE ON SCREEN

NO-SYSTEM DISK FOUND

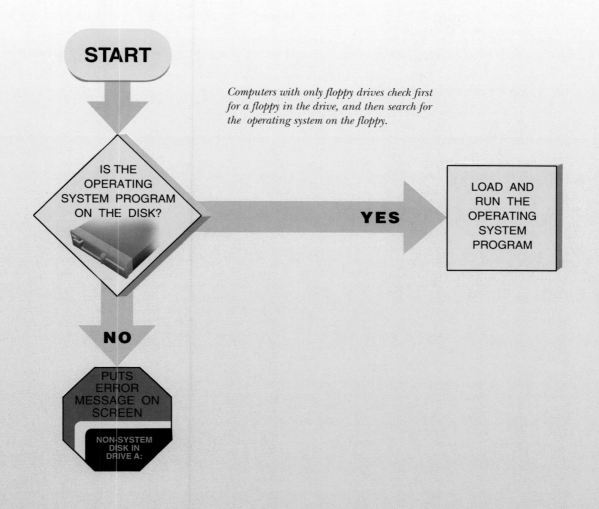

START

Computers with only floppy drives check first for a floppy in the drive, and then search for the operating system on the floppy.

IS THE OPERATING SYSTEM PROGRAM ON THE DISK?

YES

LOAD AND RUN THE OPERATING SYSTEM PROGRAM

NO

PUTS ERROR MESSAGE ON SCREEN

NON-SYSTEM DISK IN DRIVE A:

FACTS

Many of the earliest IBM PCs were actually shipped without any disk drives. To make these machines useful, there was an entire BASIC language interpreter in the original IBM BIOS. If the system could not find a disk drive with a disk in it, it ran the BASIC interpreter instead, allowing people to write programs and save them on an attached cassette tape drive.

THE OPERATING SYSTEM ADAPTS TO YOU

The same operating system gets shipped out in boxes to millions of people. However, it has to be adaptable to the needs of many different machines being operated by many different users.

Once the operating system is loaded—before it starts allowing the user control—it reads the contents of some special files. These files are designed to allow you to customize the operating system to your hardware and your way of operating.

In MS-DOS (the most common PC operating system), the file used to tell the computer how to deal with special I/O devices, and where the user can supply special ways for dealing with standard devices, is CONFIG.SYS.

```
REM A sample CONFIG.SYS
REM       These "REM" lines are REMARKS, us
REM       to people reading the file. The c

REM       MS-DOS doesn't deal comfortably w
REM       of memory. The next two lines sta
REM       which are programs that let the s
REM       interface with a special device,
REM       memory.
DEVICE=C:\DOS\HIMEM.SYS
DEVICE=C:\DOS\EMM386.EXE   RAM  HIGHSCAN  WI

REM       The system sets some RAM space as
REM       the disk drives. These two lines
REM        much room to set aside.
BUFFERS=17
FILES=50

REM       There's all sorts of other stuff
REM       into specifically, but each of th
REM       operating system and its dealing
REM       way.
DOS=UMB
LASTDRIVE=P
FCBS=4,0
DEVICEHIGH  /L:1,12048  =C:\DOS\SETVER.EXE
STACKS=0,0
DEVICE=\DEVSWAP.COM
SHELL=C:\ndos.COM  C:\DOS\      /P
DOS=HIGH
[COMMON]

REM       This loads a special driver to ma
REM       treat a normal device in a specia
REM       commercial program which sets asi
REM       disk where it *compresses* files,
REM       store more information in less sp
DEVICEHIGH  /L:1,67584  =C:\STACKER\STACHIG
```

```
REM  Things can go wrong easily with compressed files, so
REM  this runs a program to check those files every time the
REM  computer is turned on.
c:\STACKER\CHECK /WP

REM  The SET commands sets *system variables*, storing information
REM  in RAM under certain names. Programs needing that
REM  information can ask for it by name.
SET BLASTER=A220 I7 D1 T2
SET CPAV=d:\NOVIRUS\CPAV.INI
SET PCTOOLS=d:\PCTOOLS\DATA
SET SOUND=F:\SBPRO
SET GMKW5=E:\GMKW
SET TEMP=C:\WINDOWS\TEMP

REM  The PATH command tells the operating system where to look
REM  for programs that aren't in the current directory.
PATH C:\;C:\DOS;D:\NU;C:\WINDOWS;c:\windows\system;C:\;d:\UTIL

REM  The LH command runs programs in the tricky parts of memory
REM  over the 640K that DOS deals with comfortably. The programs
REM  that it is running here are more device drivers, although a
REM  slightly different type than those loaded in CONFIG.SYS
LH /L:0 C:\DOS smatdrv.exe c j k l m n o 1024 1024
LH /L:1,23952 d:\star\vmode monitor
LH /L:1,23952 d:\star\vmode vesa

REM  Another device driver, this one to run the mouse.
c:\dos\mouse

REM  This changes the MS-DOS user prompt, customizing it to
REM  whatever the user wants to see.
PROMPT $P$G

REM  And then, whenever the system is turned on, it should load
REM  up the checkers-playing program!
CHECKERS
```

Batch files are programs (easily changed by the user), which are interpreted by the operating system. Generally, they're made up mostly of commands just like you would type at the DOS prompt. When you load MS-DOS, it automatically looks for the batch program AUTOEXEC.BAT, and runs that. This is a good place to put commands that will set up the system for how you like to use it.

FACTS

Most large programs now come with installation programs (usually called INSTALL.BAT or SETUP.EXE or something similar) that automatically set up their own directories on your hard disks, copy the files, etc. Many of these will alter your AUTOEXEC.BAT and CONFIG.SYS files without you knowing about it.

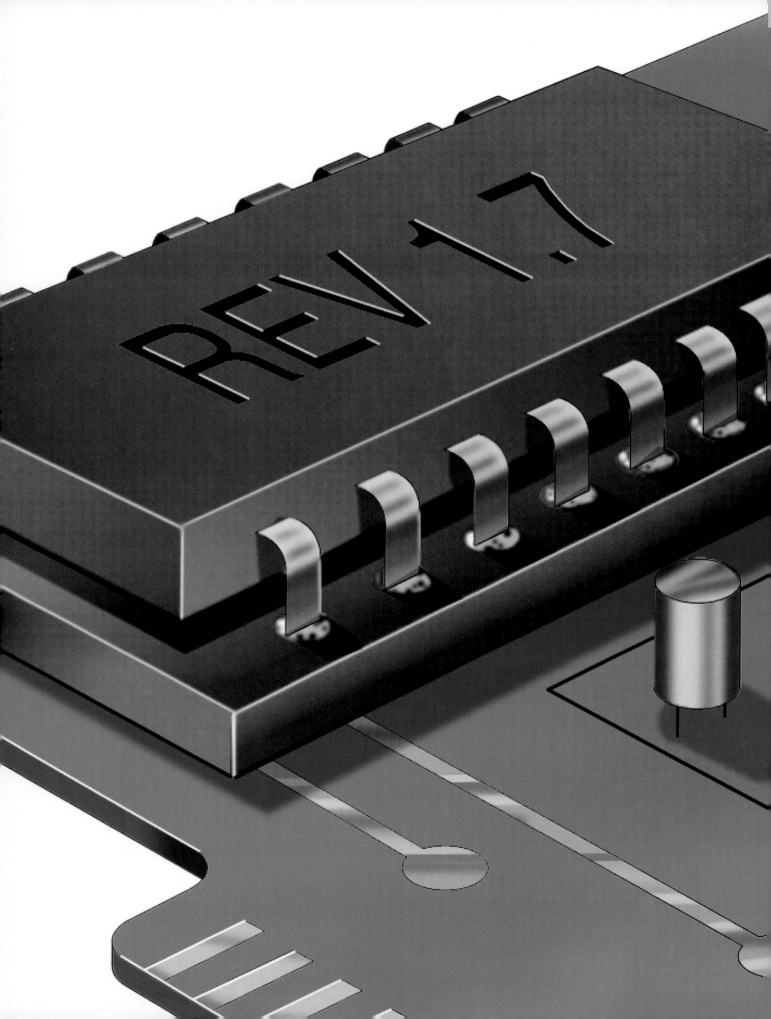

CHAPTER

5

WHAT HAPPENS WHEN YOU LOAD A PROGRAM?

Finding the File

Loading Pieces of Programs

WHAT HAPPENS WHEN YOU LOAD A PROGRAM?

Special-purpose computers can have their programs built into them—you never have to stick a floppy disk into your digital watch. Other systems, like home video game consoles, have their programs stored on big packets filled with ROM that the processor can read directly. ROM packs, however, aren't very flexible, and they are slow.

PC programs are sold on disks, which are cheap, and users either use them on floppy disks, or copy them onto the hard drives in their machine. The process of copying programs from the disk into RAM is called loading.

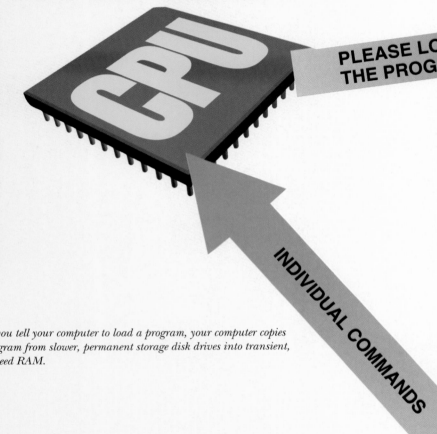

PLEASE LOAD
THE PROGRAM

INDIVIDUAL COMMANDS

When you tell your computer to load a program, your computer copies the program from slower, permanent storage disk drives into transient, high-speed RAM.

THE PROGRAM

FINDING THE FILE

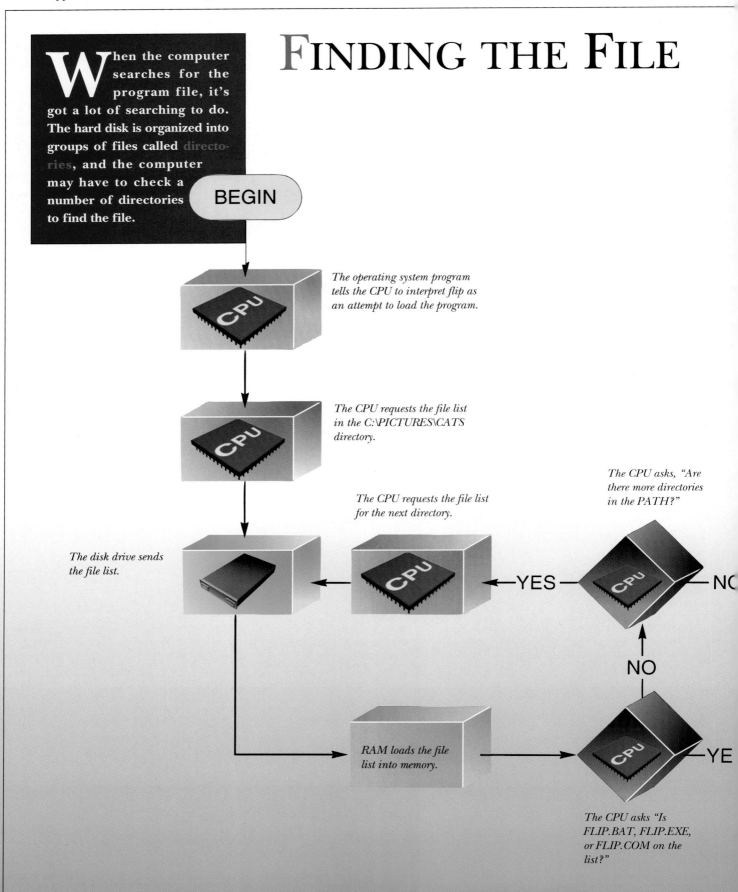

When the computer searches for the program file, it's got a lot of searching to do. The hard disk is organized into groups of files called directories, and the computer may have to check a number of directories to find the file.

BEGIN

The operating system program tells the CPU to interpret flip as an attempt to load the program.

The CPU requests the file list in the C:\PICTURES\CATS directory.

The CPU asks, "Are there more directories in the PATH?"

The CPU requests the file list for the next directory.

The disk drive sends the file list.

YES

NO

NO

RAM loads the file list into memory.

YE

The CPU asks "Is FLIP.BAT, FLIP.EXE, or FLIP.COM on the list?"

78

C:\PICTURES\CATS> flip

Let's say, for example, that you're using MS-DOS, and you want to start the program flip.

The system displays an error message.

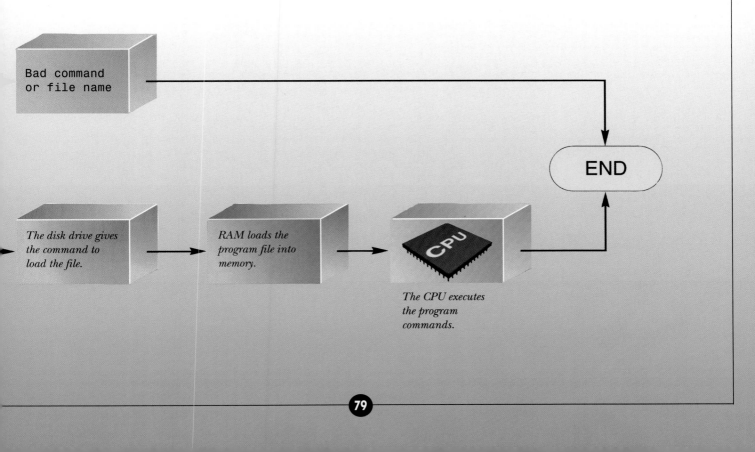

Bad command or file name

END

The disk drive gives the command to load the file.

RAM loads the program file into memory.

CPU

The CPU executes the program commands.

LOADING PIECES OF PROGRAMS

Many programs these days are huge—far too large to fit all at once in the available RAM memory on most systems. Luckily, programs can be set up to ask for further pieces of programs to be loaded in and out separately. These pieces are called overlays because the computer lays them on top of the main program.

Consider, for example, a simple word processing program. It may take more RAM than your system has to hold the main document-editing portions of the program, the document that you're editing, the spell checker portions of the program, and the printer portions of the program. Instead, the word processing program just loads up the main program, including all of the editing functions. Then, when you tell the word processing program to check your spelling, the program loads the spell checker as an overlay.

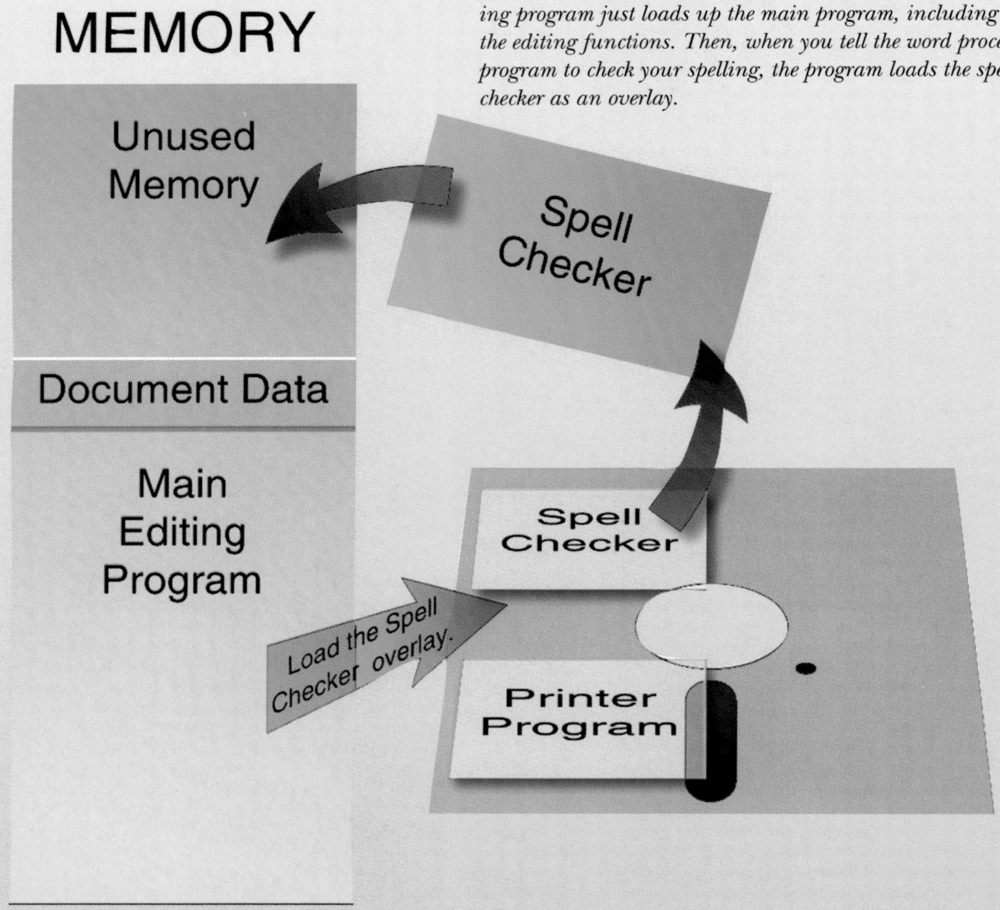

MEMORY

Unused Memory

Document Data

Main Editing Program

Spell Checker

Spell Checker

Load the Spell Checker overlay.

Printer Program

MEMORY

Spell Checker

Printer Program

Document Data

Main Editing Program

When the spell check is done and you give the command to print out the document, the printer program replaces the spell checker program in memory.

The printer program knows how to use the special functions of hundreds of printers, but it only loads the information on the printer that you're using. (This is the printer driver.)

MEMORY

Printer list

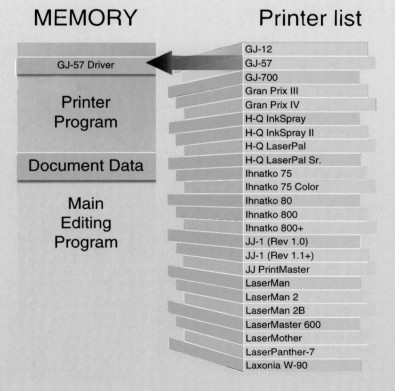

GJ-57 Driver

Printer Program

Document Data

Main Editing Program

GJ-12
GJ-57
GJ-700
Gran Prix III
Gran Prix IV
H-Q InkSpray
H-Q InkSpray II
H-Q LaserPal
H-Q LaserPal Sr.
Ihnatko 75
Ihnatko 75 Color
Ihnatko 80
Ihnatko 800
Ihnatko 800+
JJ-1 (Rev 1.0)
JJ-1 (Rev 1.1+)
JJ PrintMaster
LaserMan
LaserMan 2
LaserMan 2B
LaserMaster 600
LaserMother
LaserPanther-7
Laxonia W-90

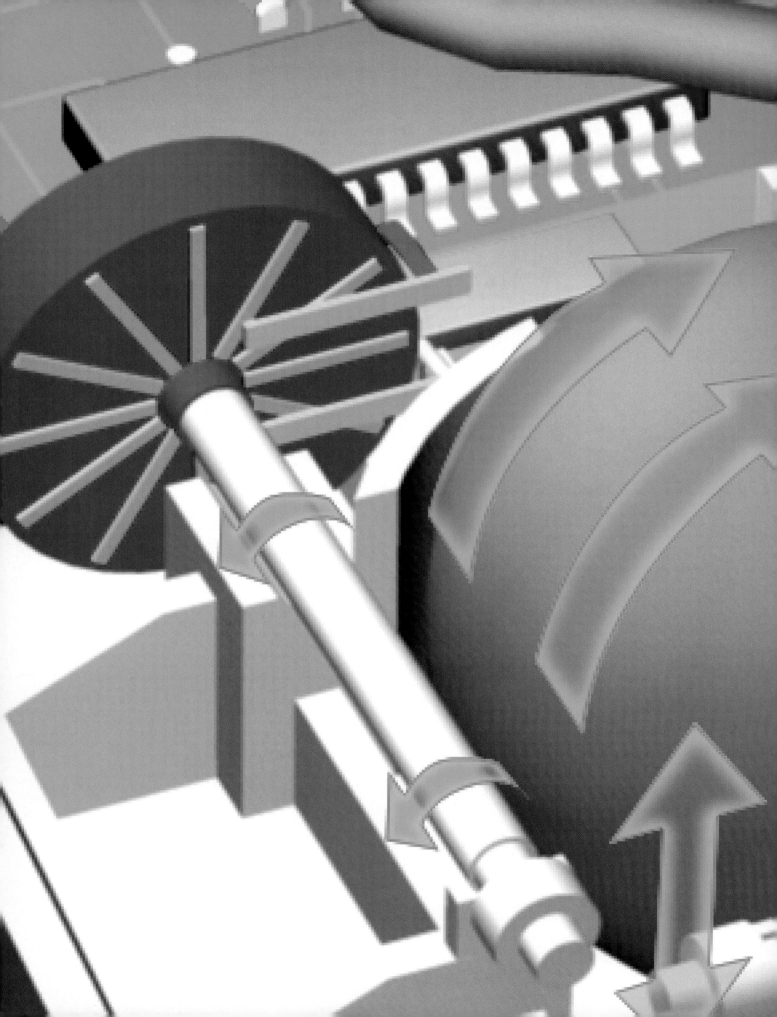

6

INPUT DEVICES

The Keyboard

The Mouse

Joysticks

INPUT DEVICES

There are a number of ways in which the user can pass commands and information to the computer—keyboards, the mouse, trackballs, and joysticks are the most common input devices but there are others. Using any one of these is actually pretty simple, but that's only because there is a lot of work going on inside the PC to make it easy.

This diagram shows a simplified version of what it takes to get your keystroke to the program that you're typing into. The process is similar for other devices.

1 *When a key is pressed...*

2 *...it gets detected by a chip inside the keyboard...*

3 *...which sends the information to a keyboard controller chip in the PC...*

4 *...which notifies the CPU...*

5 *...which checks the keyboard interrupt vector in RAM to find the keyboard program...*

6 *...that's in ROM, which says to get the key...*

7 *...from the keyboard I/O chip...*

8 *...and store it in the keystroke buffer in RAM...*

9 *...where the CPU gets it when a program asks for it.*

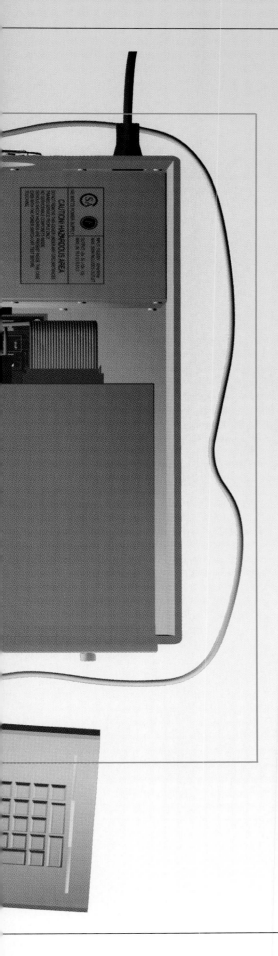

FACTS

Engineers are constantly inventing new input devices and systems. Some fade away into obscurity. Others (like the digitizing tablet) establish themselves strongly into the special niches they are designed for. And still others (like voice recognition) may well point the way for the future of computing.

A **digitizing tablet** is a special flat pad used by people using computer art programs. The pad detects where a pen-like stylus touches it, and relates that to a location on-screen. The artist draws on the pad with the stylus, and the drawing appears instantly on the screen.

A **touch screen** is a special type of monitor that can detect where your finger touches the screen. The effect is the same as with the light pen. The touch screen is less precise than the light pen, but easier to use in applications where anyone can walk up and use it, since touching the screen is very intuitive. (Many automatic teller machines use touch screens.)

Voice recognition systems turn spoken words into commands that the computer can understand. Because human speech is not clean, precise, and digital, this is very difficult for a computer to do.

THE KEYBOARD

What is there to say about the keyboard? That it's the most frequently used input device? Of course it is. That it has a lot of keys on it? It sure does. That it's not as good for smashing spiders as a phone book? Absolutely.

To the user, the keyboard is just a keyboard. Inside, though, there's a whole lot of mechanical and electronic pieces doing their little mechanical and electronic jobs.

Every key on the keyboard is linked to a switch on the circuit. A chip inside the keyboard constantly scans every circuit and, if the switch opens or closes, passes that information along to the PC.

On a membrane keyboard, pressing a key pushes contacts together, allowing electricity to flow through the circuit.

On a *mechanical keyboard*, pressing a key separates contacts, stopping electricity which is generally flowing through the circuit. The spring keeps the key in the up position.

FACTS

The keyboard sends a message every time a key is pressed, and another one when you take your finger off the key and it springs back up. This way, the PC can tell when you're holding a key down.

Some programs allow you to change what each key on your keyboard stands for. They intercept the key value received by your PC and remap it with a different key. This is handy for people who are used to different keyboard layouts.

The original PC keyboard had a full typewriter key set, plus a pad of number keys that also doubled as cursor keys, plus ten function keys that programs could use for their own special purposes.

The most common keyboard design today is the 101-key enhanced keyboard, which has all of the keys of the original, plus two more function keys, plus a group of cursor keys, plus nine keys dedicated to special functions.

Also available are compact or space-saver keyboards, which do not have the number pad. These are cheaper and take up less table space, but for number-intensive uses it really is a lot easier to have a number pad than to be using the row of numbers above the letter keys.

THE MOUSE

The mouse is a device used to position a cursor or pointer on-screen. Using a mouse is easy—when you slide the mouse left across the table or mouse pad, the pointer moves left on-screen. Slide it to the right, the pointer moves right. Pushing the mouse forward or back causes the pointer to move up or down.

This makes the mouse much more instinctive and precise than cursor keys. With cursor keys, you tell the computer what direction to move the cursor. With a mouse, you aren't giving the computer a direction, you're giving it an exact position to place a cursor or pointer.

The mouse also has buttons on the top, which programs use in different ways. In a paint program, for example, the left button might start drawing where the pointer points to, while the right button might erase the drawing.

The common mechanical mouse has a ball on the bottom. When you slide the mouse, the ball rolls against rollers inside the mouse, one roller picking up the side-to-side movement, the other picking up the up-and-down. The rollers are on axles, each with an encoder wheel. By telling how fast and how far those wheels are turning, the system can tell how fast and how far you have moved the mouse.

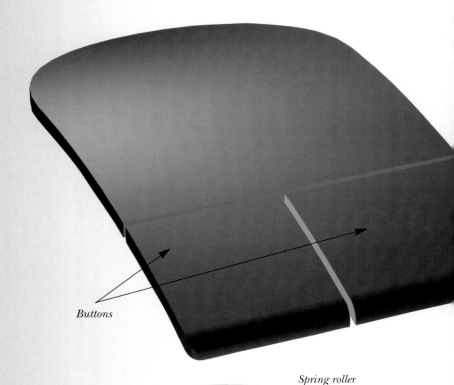

Buttons

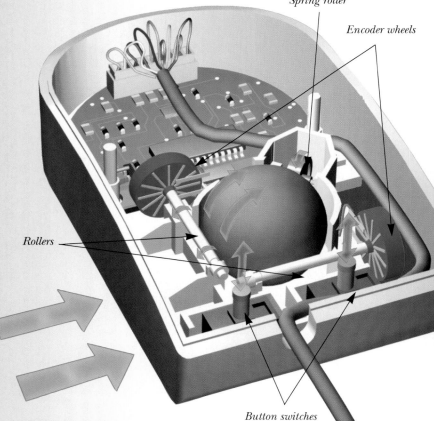

Spring roller

Encoder wheels

Rollers

Button switches

The usual mouse has plastic wheels with metal strips. These strips complete circuits with leads that are hanging nearby. By tracking when these wires complete the circuits, the mouse can tell how fast and far it is being moved.

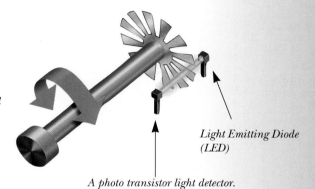

An opti-mechanical mouse tracks a slotted wheel interrupting a beam of light to tell how fast and far the mouse is moving.

Light Emitting Diode (LED)

A photo transistor light detector.

An optical mouse doesn't have a ball on the bottom. Instead, you slide it across a special reflective pad with a grid painted on it. Lights reflect off the pad, so the mouse can tell when it is sliding across the grid.

A trackball is basically an upside-down opti-mechanical mouse. You roll the ball directly with your hand, instead of sliding it against the table. This way, you don't need open table space to use it, so it is very handy for laptop computers.

FACTS

The mouse got its name because its lumpy shape and cable "tail" reminded people of a rodent. However, new wireless mice don't have the tail. They use infrared to send information about the mouse position and the buttons to a receiver unit, the same way a TV remote control sends signals to a TV set.

Most mice have two or three buttons, which programs will use for functions related to where the mouse is pointing. Some have more buttons, with drive software that lets those buttons act like certain keys on the keyboard, so that people who use the mouse can give certain commands without removing their hand from the mouse.

JOYSTICKS

A joystick is a simple, limited controller used mainly for playing games. The basic joystick design is a tiltable rod sticking out of a pad, with a couple of buttons attached somewhere. With that basic design philosophy, a wide array of different shaped joysticks have been produced. Different players playing different games have very different needs, and the joystick that feels right for one person who is using a flight simulator may feel very wrong to someone else who is playing Revenge Of The Martian Space Bunnies From Venus.

Moving the joystick moves two metal leads against electronic devices called variable resistors. A variable resistor allows different amounts of current to pass through depending on where the lead is placed against it. The amount of current is high at one end, and low at the other. (A light dimmer switch is a good example of a variable resistor that you see in action.)

One of the resistors tracks the side-to-side movement. The other tracks the up-and-down movement. These two components of the joystick's position are referred to as the X-axis and Y-axis, respectively.

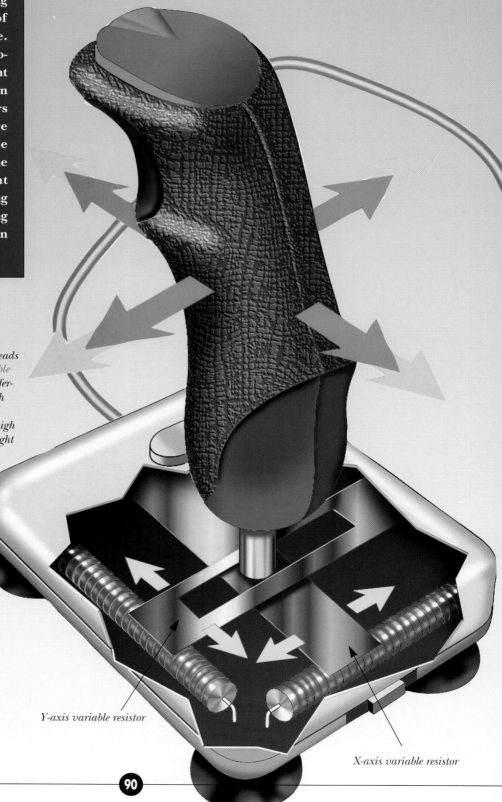

Y-axis variable resistor

X-axis variable resistor

FACTS

For the advanced user of flight simulation programs, there are a number of controllers available which look and move like modern aircraft control wheels.

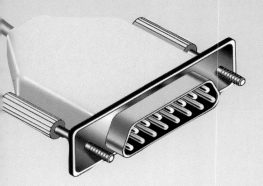

The 15 pin sockets the joystick cables plug into are rarely built into the machine. You can get special cards called game adapters *that provide these sockets, and some cards designed for other purposes also provide these sockets, called* game ports.

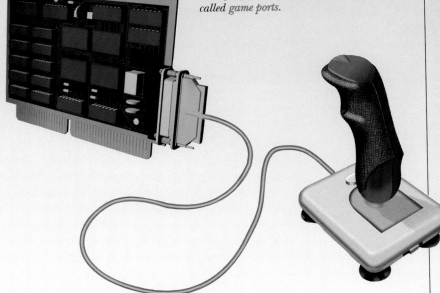

WHAT HAPPENS WHEN FILES ARE CREATED?

WHAT HAPPENS WHEN FILES ARE CREATED?

If you take every piece of information that you need to store and just throw it on a pile, with no markings and no way of telling one piece from another, you would never find anything. Your tax records would be mixed in with your phone number lists, and they might be buried under the directions to operate your VCR, your car insurance papers, and the recipe for cheeseburger pie.

In order to keep things straight, you might put together a filing system, with each item in its own file, marked with a label explaining what it is. It should come as no surprise that with the amount of information that the computer stores on disk, it needs its own organizational system. It doesn't use physical file folders and pieces of paper, but the ideas are very much the same.

The organizational system is so much like using file drawers that each storage unit is called a file.

Each individual program, each word processing document, each database, each drawing, and each other grouping of data has its own file, with its own name.

Additionally, there are some files which hold groups of other files. These files are called directories.

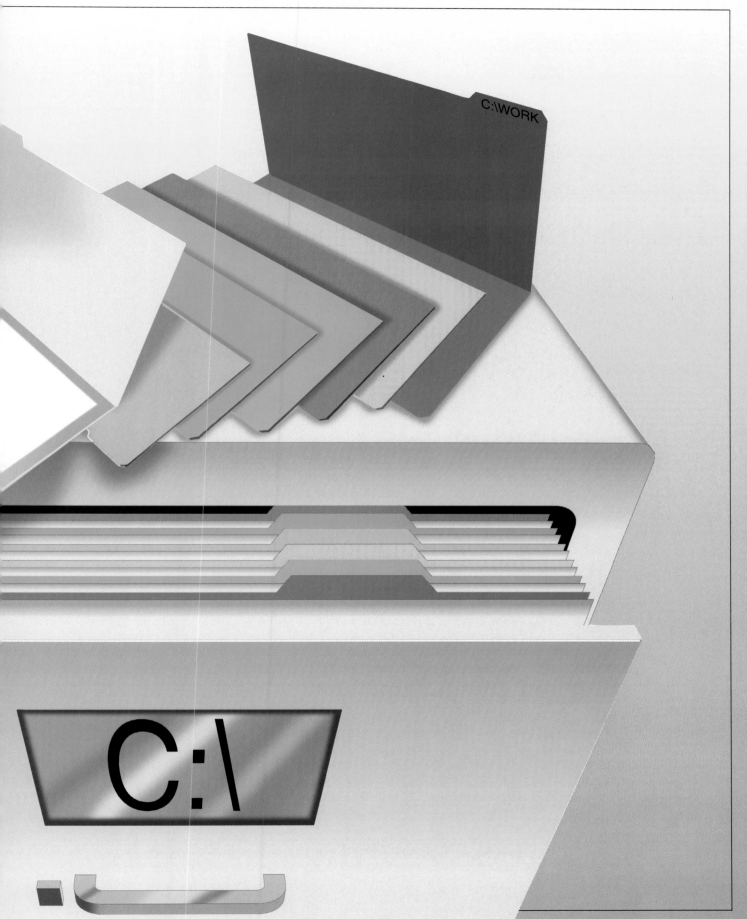

TYPES OF FILES

There are two types of information files: **program files**, which store lists of commands designed to get the system to perform a specific function, and **data files**, which store information for the programs to process.

The filing system treats all information files the same. The portions of the operating system that handle keeping the file system straight don't pay attention to the purpose of that information.

```
WordMaster Rev 2.3                    File: ILOVEU

To whom it may concern:
      I love you. Ever since we first met at Jeff's party, I'v
been haunted by your eyes, whatever color they are, and the l
flesh tones of your skin.
      If you would only be willing to be mine, forever, then p
fill out the enclosed form, stating your name, phone number,
hours that you will be available from now until the end of ti
A postage paid envelope has been enclosed for your convenienc
      Thank you for your time.


      Yours possibly _




Ln: 10  Pos:32
```

When stored on a disk, the word processing document (with a name like ILOVEU.WP), will be considered a data file. Most of the files you create will be data files.

Whether the file is a program or a data file, it's really stored as just a big long string of binary numbers. The word processing program file is a string of numbers the CPU interprets as commands which make up a word processing program. The love letter file is a list of numbers which the word processing program interprets as the letter.

1·0·1·0·1·0·0

FACTS

MS-DOS limits what you can use as a file name. Each file name can have up to eight characters, followed by a period, followed by up to three more characters (called the file extension). Any letters in lowercase will automatically be changed to uppercase.

The file extension is generally used to indicate the type of file. All program files, for example, must have the extension EXE, COM, or BAT, or the operating system will not recognize them as programs. Many programs that create data files tag them with a special extension all their own, to make it easy for both the program and the user to recognize the file as belonging to that program. A spreadsheet, for example, might name the worksheet files it creates with the extension WRK. That way, you know that it's a worksheet file for that spreadsheet program.

When using a program that does not pick the file extension for you, it's a good idea to come up with a file extension standard that is meaningful to you.

The commands that turn the computer into a word processor are a program, and are stored in a program file. That program will come with some data files (special information which it needs). When the word processor checks the spelling on your document, for example, it's using a data file that has a list of correctly spelled words. Data files that come with a program are called support files.

Files are kept in groups called directories. By devoting a directory to files that are somehow related to each other (like a directory of word processing letters), it makes it easier to find a given file.

```
Files in C:\WORDMSTR\LETTERS

BETTY           .WP
ILOVEU          .WP
IOWEU           .WP
IRIS            .WP
JANE            .WP
JULIE           .WP
MOM                    <DIR>
PATRICIA        .WP
SARAH           .WP
UOWEME          .WP
```

You can even store directories within other directories.

HOW DIRECTORIES ARE ORGANIZED

The directories keep groups of files organized in a way that makes it easy to find what you're looking for—if you take proper advantage of them. Many people give little thought to their directory structures and file names, giving files cryptic names and leaving them in the midst of a huge directory. This makes it difficult to find a given file if that file name isn't memorized.

```
Files in C:\
ACE      .BAT
AUTOEXEC.BAT
COMMAND .COM
CONFIG  .SYS
DOS              <DIR>
FRED     .BAK
GAMES            <DIR>
GENIUS  .
RUNME    .EXE
SPREADER.EXE
VIEW     .COM
WM       .BAT
WM       .OLD
WORDMSTR         <DIR>
```

```
Files in C:\GAMES
BUNNIES          <DIR>
CARDS            <DIR>
CHESSGOD         <DIR>
FANTASY          <DIR>
SHOOTUPS         <DIR>
SPACEGMS         <DIR>
TWIZZLER         <DIR>
```

```
Files in C:\WORDMSTR
ARTICLES         <DIR>
INSTALL .BAT
LETTERS          <DIR>
POEMS            <DIR>
README  .
WM       .EXE
WM       .DOC    <DIR>
WORDMSTR.DOC
WORDMSTR.EXE
WORDMSTR.OVL
```

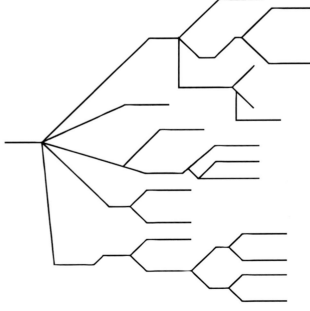

Because the directory structure branches out— with subdirectories having their own subdirec- tories—the entire directory structure of a disk is sometimes called a directory tree.

The root directory can have directories in it, and those directories can hold other directories, and so on. A directory that is in another directory is called a sub-directory.

Every disk has a first, primary directory, called the root directory.

```
es in C:\GAMES\BUNNIES          Files in C:\WORDMSTR\LETTERS\MOM
NIES .EXE                       APRIL07 .WP
NIES .LV1                       APRIL09 .WP
NIES .LV2                       APRIL12 .WP
NIES .LV3                       APRIL13 .WP
NIES .LV4                       APRIL25 .WP
RES  .HI                        APRIL30 .WP
                                AUGUST1 .WP
                                AUGUST7 .WP
es in C:\WORDMSTR\LETTERS       FEB12   .WP
TY   .WP                        FEB15   .WP
VEU  .WP ◄                      FEB22   .WP
EU   .WP                        FEB28   .WP
S    .WP                        JULY01  .WP
E    .WP                        JULY03  .WP
IE   .WP                        JULY17  .WP
                                JULY24  .WP
             <DIR>              JULY25  .WP
RICIA.WP                        JULY29  .WP
AH   .WP                        JUNE02  .WP
EME  .WP                        JUNE10  .WP
                                JUNE12  .WP
es in C:\WORDMSTR\POEMS          JUNE18  .WP
TA   .ODE                       JUNE28  .WP
CA   .ODE                       JUNE29  .WP
CHELLE.ODE                      MARCH01 .WP
NCY  .ODE                       MARCH04 .WP
NTUCKT.LIM                      MARCH05 .WP
ERLEY .ODE                      MARCH12 .WP
                                MARCH14 .WP
es in C:\WORDMSTR\WM.DOC         MARCH21 .WP
RDMSTR.DOC                      MARCH31 .WP
                                MAY07   .WP
                                MAY12   .WP
                                MAY14   .WP
                                MAY19   .WP
                                MAY22   .WP
                                MAY27   .WP
```

When using DOS, one directory at a time is your current directory, where DOS looks for files unless otherwise specified. At any time, you can refer to any file by listing the disk letter (followed by a colon), followed by a list of the directories and subdirectories it takes to access that file. The root directory is named with just the backslash (\) character; directories under that are listed with their names separated by the \.

If you group your files too specifically, it can be cumbersome just specifying the directory you are seeking.

Full file name is
C:\WORDMSTR\LETTERS\ILOVEU.WP

SECTIONS OF THE DISK

The space on a disk is broken up into sectors. Each sector on a disk holds the same amount of data: 512 bytes, or half a kilobyte (1,024 bytes).

Sectors are grouped into clusters. Every cluster on the disk has the same number of sectors, although how many sectors that is varies, depending on the type of disk. These clusters are used to store the actual information in the files, as well as storing subdirectories.

DOS, Windows, and some OS/2 systems work this way. Other operating systems handle things differently, but with many of the same concepts.

The first sector is the boot block. This sector stores the boot program that tells the computer how to find the operating system.

The next group of sectors stores the file allocation table. The File Allocation Table (FAT) keeps track of what parts of the disks are used.

The FAT is so important that a second copy of the table is kept. If the two copies aren't the same, the system knows that something has gone wrong with the disk.

BOOT BLOCK

FAT

BACKUP FAT

ROOT DIRECTORY

These sectors are known together as the system area.

The next bunch of sectors stores the root directory, a list of names of files and subdirectories, and information about where those files are on the disk.

CLUSTER 2

CLUSTER 3

CLUSTER 4

Each cluster is numbered, starting with number 2. While a file or subdirectory may take up any number of clusters, each cluster can only hold information for one file. Even if there are only a few bytes of information in a file, it will still take up the entire cluster, and the rest of the cluster remains empty.

All of the sectors not used for the system area are called the file area.

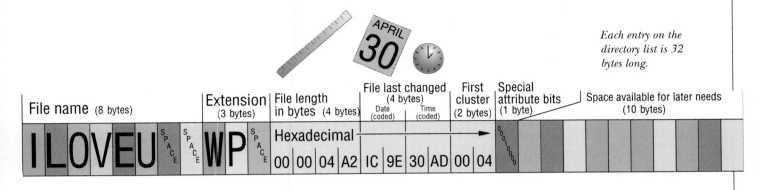

File name (8 bytes)		Extension (3 bytes)	File length in bytes (4 bytes)	File last changed (4 bytes) Date (coded) Time (coded)	First cluster (2 bytes)	Special attribute bits (1 byte)	Space available for later needs (10 bytes)
I LOVEU SPACE SPACE	WP SPACE		Hexadecimal 00 00 04 A2	IC 9E 30 AD	00 04	00010000	

Each entry on the directory list is 32 bytes long.

Each spot in the FAT stores information about a given cluster on the disk. (This example uses two bytes per entry, like most hard disk FATs. Floppy disks use a byte and a half per entry.)

The file that starts in cluster 4 continues in cluster 5, and from there to cluster 9.

This code means that this is the last cluster for this file.

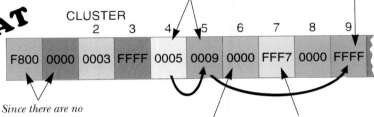

FAT

CLUSTER
2 3 4 5 6 7 8 9

F800 0000 0003 FFFF 0005 0009 0000 FFF7 0000 FFFF

Since there are no clusters numbered 0 or 1, the first two slots in the FAT are used to store information about the disk format.

This cluster is empty and can be used.

This is a special code for faulty disk areas. This will keep the system from trying to use this area of the disk.

FACTS

Because the root directory is a fixed size, there is a limit to how many files it can store.

Subdirectories are stored like other files, and can expand to take up as many clusters as are available. As such, a subdirectory only runs out of room when you have run out of room on the disk.

The file attribute bits mark special information about the file, like whether the file has been backed up since it was last changed, or if the file is supposed to be hidden from directory-reading commands, or if the file actually is a subdirectory. Some of these bits are set aside for the future.

CREATING A FILE

Most programs create a file at some time or another. Rather than having to build the full set of commands to handle this into each program, the job of creating a new file is left to the operating system, and each individual program needs only send a single command to the operating system.

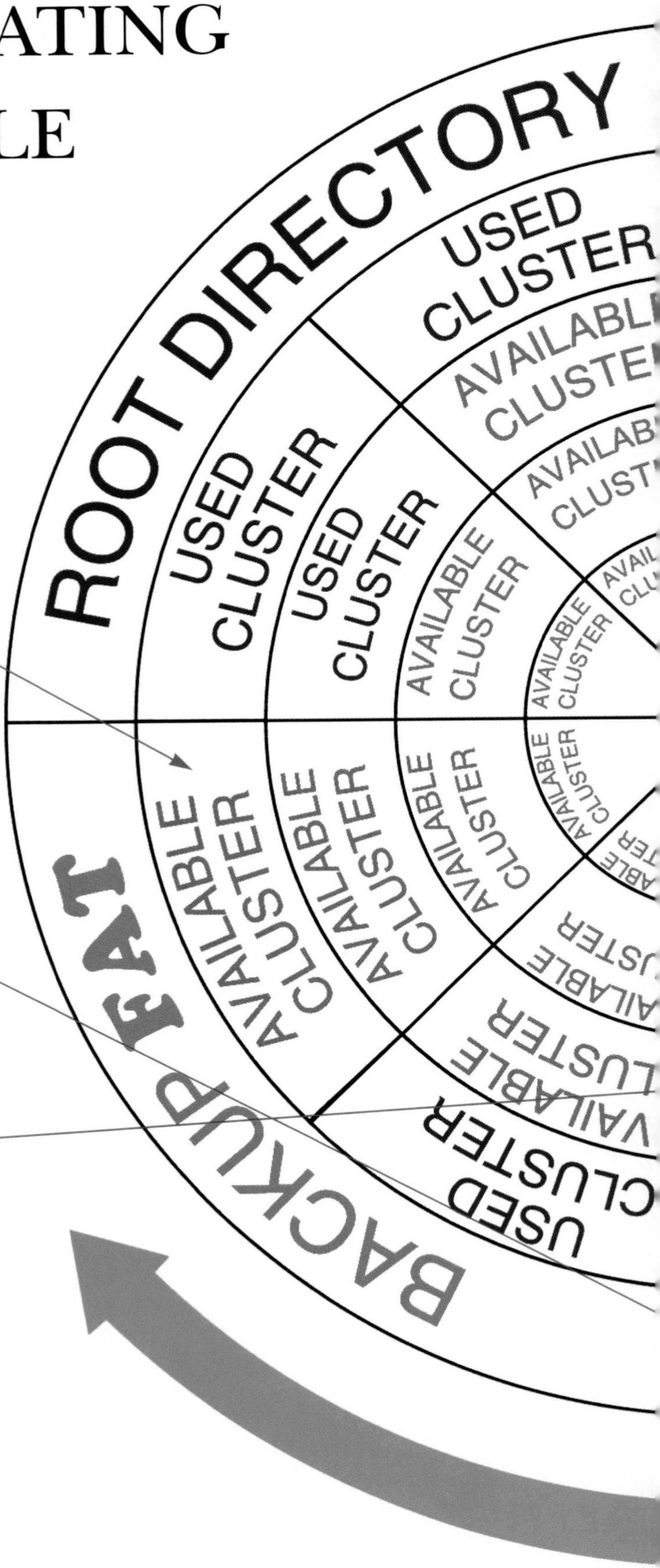

6 *It fills up that cluster, and repeats this process until it has completed writing the file.*

7 *Then it writes the "end of file" code in the FAT slot for the last cluster…*

8 *…and puts the file length in the directory.*

ROOT DIRECTORY

BACKUP FAT

USED CLUSTER

USED CLUSTER

USED CLUSTER

AVAILABLE CLUSTER

AVAILABLE CLUSTER

AVAILABLE CLUSTER

AVAILABLE CLUSTER

AVAILABLE CLUSTER

AVAILABLE CLUSTER

AVAILABLE CLUSTER

AVAILABLE CLUSTER

AVAILABLE CLUSTER

AVAILABLE CLUSTER

AVAILABLE CLUSTER

USED CLUSTER

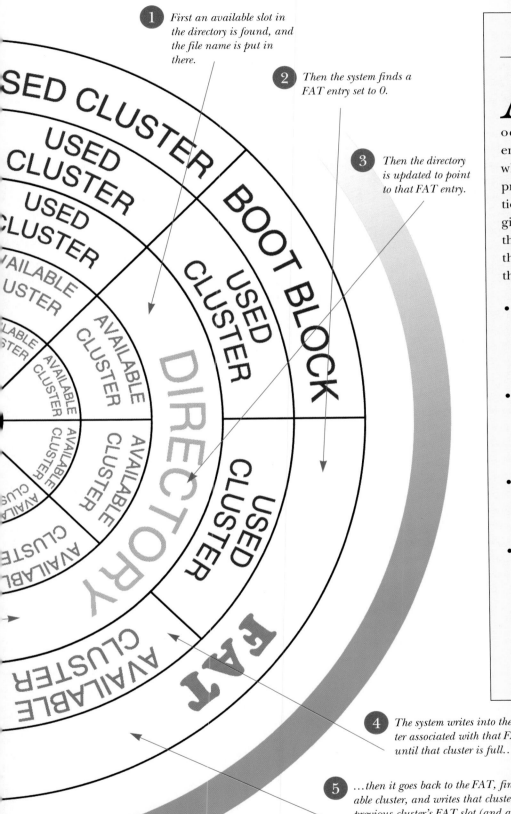

1 First an available slot in the directory is found, and the file name is put in there.

2 Then the system finds a FAT entry set to 0.

3 Then the directory is updated to point to that FAT entry.

4 The system writes into the cluster associated with that FAT until that cluster is full...

5 ...then it goes back to the FAT, finds another available cluster, and writes that cluster's number in the previous cluster's FAT slot (and a copy in the duplicate FAT as well).

FACTS

A number of things can go wrong when you try to save a file. If one of them occurs, DOS will generate an error code or message indicating what went wrong. A well-made program will pass on the information about what went wrong and give you a chance to try to adjust the problem before trying to save the file again. Here are some of the most common problems:

- *Full disk.* When all of the clusters are already used for files, there's no more space to write a new file.

- *Unknown directory.* You specified that the file be put in a subdirectory that the system could not find.

- *No disk in drive.* This can often happen if you forget to close the door of a floppy disk drive.

- *Full directory.* This only happens when you are writing to the root directory. While the root directory is rather large, it is still possible to fill it up, particularly if you are not taking care to organize your files into easily-handled subdirectories.

COPYING AND MOVING FILES

There are many reasons for copying files. You may want to give someone a copy of a file from your hard disk, so you copy it onto a floppy. Or, you may want to work on rewriting a story, so you copy the original file under a different name, so that if you don't like the changes, you still have the original.

Moving a file happens less frequently—generally, you move a file when you are organizing a disk, and find that you want a file in a different directory than you have it in, or if you want to take a file off of one disk and put it onto another.

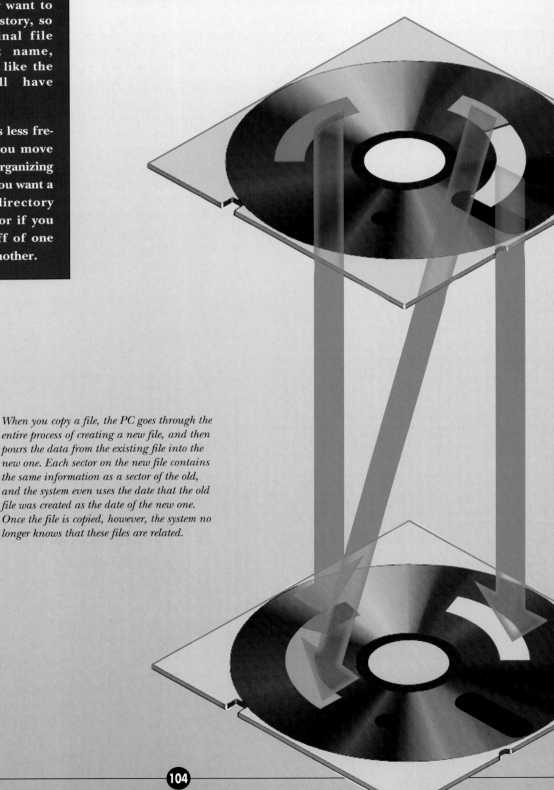

When you copy a file, the PC goes through the entire process of creating a new file, and then pours the data from the existing file into the new one. Each sector on the new file contains the same information as a sector of the old, and the system even uses the date that the old file was created as the date of the new one. Once the file is copied, however, the system no longer knows that these files are related.

When you move a file from one disk to another,
the system simply copies *the file*, and then
deletes *the original*.

\WORDMSTR\LETTERS

BETTY^{SPACE SPACE SPACE}	WP^{SPACE}	. . .
ILOVEU^{SPACE SPACE}	WP^{SPACE}	. . .
IOWEU^{SPACE SPACE SPACE}	WP^{SPACE}	. . .
IRIS^{SPACE SPACE SPACE SPACE}	WP^{SPACE}	. . .
JANE^{SPACE SPACE SPACE SPACE}	WP^{SPACE}	. . .

\FINANCE

BILLS^{SPACE SPACE SPACE}	LST^{SPACE}	. . .
CREDIT^{SPACE SPACE}	WP^{SPACE}	. . .

When you move a file to another directory on the same
disk, the computer doesn't actually move the file at all.
Instead, it just invalidates the directory entry from the
old directory and places the same entry in the new directory. The file information is still in the same clusters, it's
just that this new directory entry points to it.

DELETING A FILE

There are many times when you might want to delete a file on your disk. Generally, it's a file that you don't need any more, and rather than have that file take up disk space and clutter up your directory, you just get rid of it.

The newer versions of DOS have an option to not really delete files immediately, but to just move them to a special "deleted file" holding area for a while, and then delete them later. This is so you can get the file back if you accidentally delete it. But what we deal with here is what happens when the file really gets deleted.

1 *Let's say that you wanted to delete the file ILOVEU.WP. First, just the first character of the directory entry is eliminated.*

B	E	T	T	Y	SPACE	SPACE	SPACE	W	P	SPACE	...
I	L	O	V	E	U	SPACE	SPACE	W	P	SPACE	...
I	R	I	S	SPACE	SPACE	SPACE	SPACE	W	P	SPACE	...

2 *In place of the ASCII code for the first letter is put a hexadecimal value 5E, which doesn't stand for any letter. This lets the system know the directory space is open.*

| Hex 5E | L | O | V | E | U | SPACE | SPACE | W | P | SPACE | ... |

3 *Then the system goes through the FAT (and the duplicate FAT) and zeros out the slots for all of the clusters that the file had occupied. (Notice that another file has been written in clusters 6 and 8, and these are not affected by the erasure of the ILOVEU.WP file.)*

FAT

| CLUSTER | | 0008 | FFF7 | FFFF | |
| 4 | 5 | 6 | 7 | 8 | 9 |

It knows how long the file was.

Notice that the computer never bothered actually erasing the information that was in the file. The information isn't actually wiped out until another file uses those clusters. This allows for a real nifty trick: the ability to *undelete* a file that was accidentally deleted.

It knows where the first cluster of the file was.

...e system still has ...st of the file name.

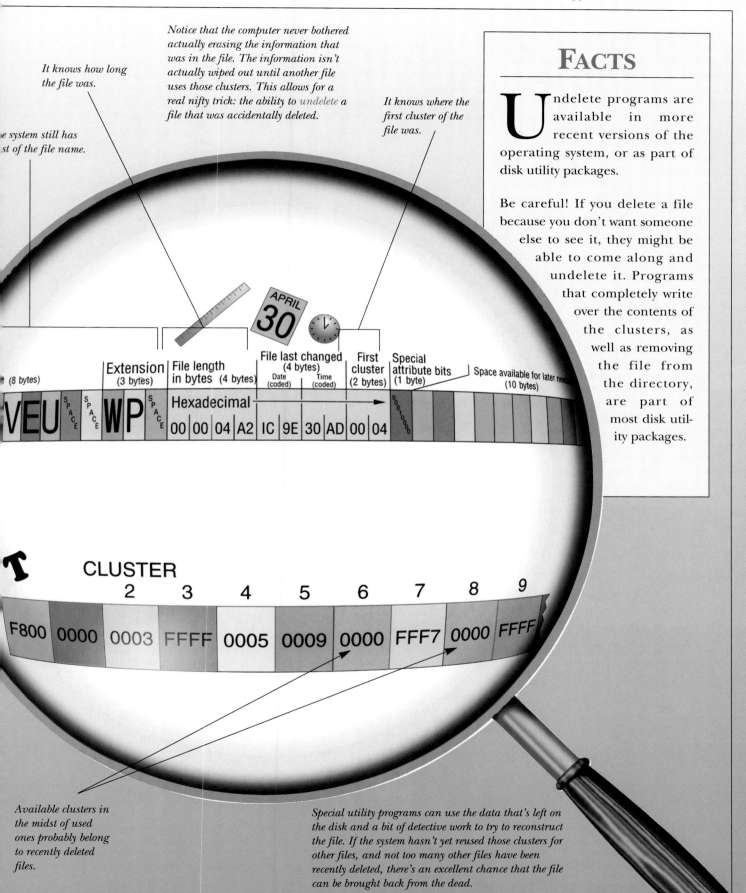

FACTS

Undelete programs are available in more recent versions of the operating system, or as part of disk utility packages.

Be careful! If you delete a file because you don't want someone else to see it, they might be able to come along and undelete it. Programs that completely write over the contents of the clusters, as well as removing the file from the directory, are part of most disk utility packages.

(8 bytes)

Extension (3 bytes)

File length in bytes (4 bytes)

File last changed (4 bytes) — Date (coded) / Time (coded)

First cluster (2 bytes)

Special attribute bits (1 byte)

Space available for later nee... (10 bytes)

VEU | SPACE | SPACE | WP | SPACE | Hexadecimal | 00 | 00 | 04 | A2 | IC | 9E | 30 | AD | 00 | 04 | 00010000

APRIL 30

CLUSTER

2 3 4 5 6 7 8 9

F800 | 0000 | 0003 | FFFF | 0005 | 0009 | 0000 | FFF7 | 0000 | FFFF

Available clusters in the midst of used ones probably belong to recently deleted files.

Special utility programs can use the data that's left on the disk and a bit of detective work to try to reconstruct the file. If the system hasn't yet reused those clusters for other files, and not too many other files have been recently deleted, there's an excellent chance that the file can be brought back from the dead.

FRAGMENTED FILES

When a file is saved, the computer stores it on the earliest available clusters. On a freshly formatted disk, this will be a number of clusters right in a row.

However, when files get deleted, they leave available clusters among the already used ones. And the next file that gets written will start by using those clusters. But that next file may only find a couple of available clusters in one spot, and then have to continue in clusters further down the disk.

Additionally, when you add more information to an already existing file, it has to grab more clusters to store the information. The first available clusters are grabbed, and these may not be anywhere near the clusters the file already uses.

When a file takes up clusters on the disk that are not right in a row, the file is considered fragmented.

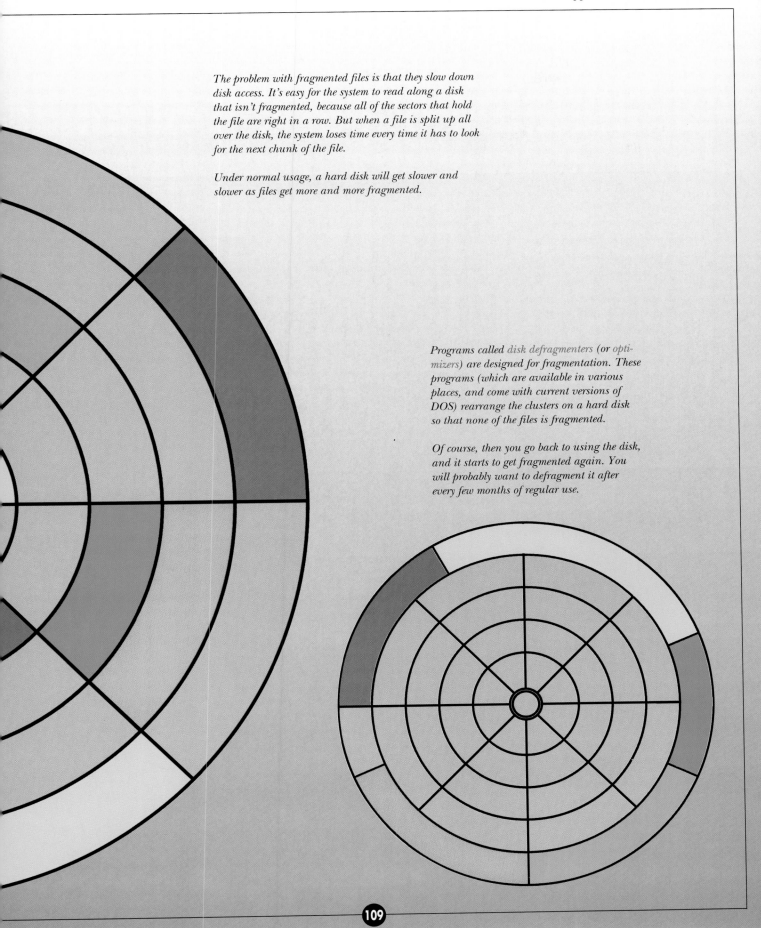

The problem with fragmented files is that they slow down disk access. It's easy for the system to read along a disk that isn't fragmented, because all of the sectors that hold the file are right in a row. But when a file is split up all over the disk, the system loses time every time it has to look for the next chunk of the file.

Under normal usage, a hard disk will get slower and slower as files get more and more fragmented.

Programs called disk defragmenters (or optimizers) are designed for fragmentation. These programs (which are available in various places, and come with current versions of DOS) rearrange the clusters on a hard disk so that none of the files is fragmented.

Of course, then you go back to using the disk, and it starts to get fragmented again. You will probably want to defragment it after every few months of regular use.

FILE COMPRESSION

Computer programs keep getting larger and larger. The hard disk that seemed so huge as to be unfillable when you bought it a couple of years back may be perilously close to running out of space.

The companies that make hard disks would like you to buy a brand new, far larger hard disk. But software companies are offering other alternatives. There have long been programs that let you squeeze files into a small space. These programs, called file compression utilities or archive utilities, are very handy for storing programs that you don't use very often, or for packing together a group of files, so that you can send them more quickly over a modem or distribute them.

More recently, there's been a lot of interest in disk compression utilities, programs that automatically squeeze files when you save them on disk and automatically unsqueeze them whenever you use them. These programs generally let you fit almost twice as much data on your hard disk, and once you set them up, you rarely will even know they are there, because everything is automatic. These are so popular that they now come bundled in with some versions of DOS.

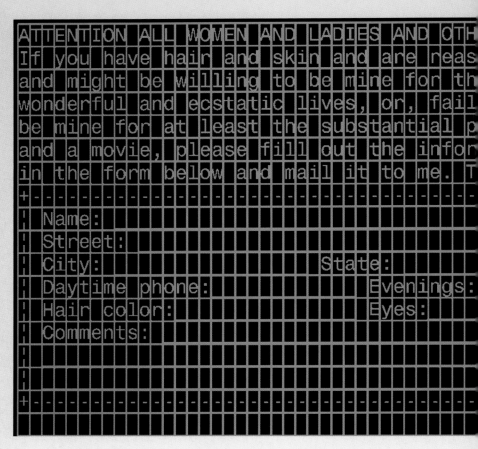

In a normal word processing file, each character takes up one byte of storage (storing the ASCII value for that character). With one byte, we can represent up to 256 different characters, but usually, we are using far less than that. If we only need to represent 26 uppercase letters, 26 lowercase letters, and a few punctuation marks, we could store each in six bits, which would allow 64 different characters.

In files, the same character is often repeated many times in a row. Compression programs replace these long repetitions with a special code like this.

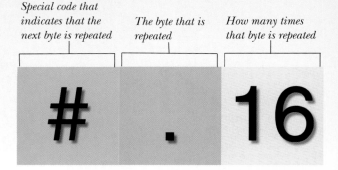

Special code that indicates that the next byte is repeated

The byte that is repeated

How many times that byte is repeated

By coming up with a six-bit code instead of ASCII, and by ignoring the usual byte boundaries, we could fit four characters into every three bytes.

```
|0|0|0|0|0|1|0|1|0|1|0|0|0|1|0|1|0|0|0|0|0|1|0|1|
     BYTE1          BYTE2          BYTE3
```

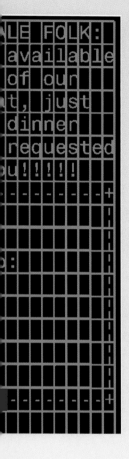

The text compression routines that are used are actually trickier than that, using fewer bits for common letters like E and T, and less for things like Q and Z. But the concept is the same.

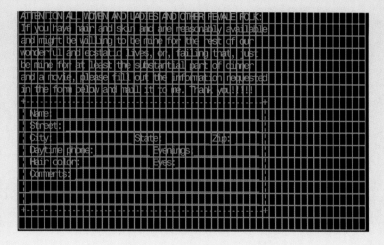

This way, the information can be stored in a smaller space, but it is easy for the computer to exactly reconstruct the original file.

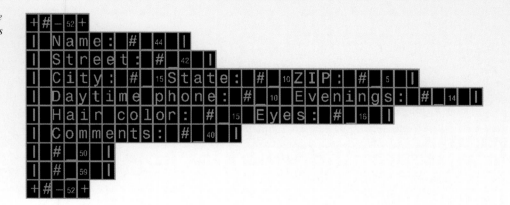

The disk compression utility takes up what looks like a *huge* *file* on the hard disk, and pretends that it is a separate disk drive.

Whenever the system tries to read from or write to that phantom disk drive, the disk compression program intervenes and handles that information itself.

Because the disk compression program has its own method of handling files, it doesn't leave empty space at the end of a cluster for files that don't fill up a whole cluster. This saves a lot of space.

COMPRESSED BETTY.WP	CLUSTER 2
COMPRESSED ILOVEU.WP	
COMPRESSED IOWEU.WP	CLUSTER 3
COMPRESSED SHERLEY.WP	CLUSTER 4

FACTS

Disk compression programs count on other programs going properly through the operating system to read and write files. Programs that "cheat" and try to work outside the operating system (like most disk utilities, for example) have a problem dealing with compressed disks because they won't know how to find and decompress the files.

It would seem like having to do all that work compressing and decompressing files would slow the system down. However, by dealing with smaller files, the time saved on reading from and writing to the disk more than makes up for the time spent compressing and decompressing. Your system may actually run faster working with a compressed disk.

The compression/decompression program sits in memory at all times, taking up some RAM space. Plus, there is occasional special maintenance that should be done on compressed drives. All in all, though, most people find disk compression well worth using.

8

WHAT HAPPENS WHEN YOU USE YOUR DISK DRIVES?

WHAT HAPPENS WHEN YOU USE YOUR DISK DRIVES?

Data storage systems come in many varieties, each trying to fill mass storage needs in different ways. And they each have different strengths and weaknesses in terms of speed, cost, writability, and ability to handle commercially distributed program and data packages. Most of them involve storing information on a spinning disk of some sort of matter, so the machinery to spin the disk and read and write information on it is called a disk drive.

Controller boards translate the CPU commands into a language appropriate for the individual type of device.

The CPU talks to most types of mass storage devices using a common language. It treats them all just as devices.

③ *Electronics on the device itself turn those commands into physical control of the storage device.*

FACTS

Even for a given type of device, there may be different languages available for communication between the controller and device. Hard disks, for example, usually communicate with their controller using IDE, the Integrated Drive Electronics standard. However, the Small Computer Systems Interface (or SCSI) standard is gaining popularity. (SCSI is pronounced "skuzzy," although one computer manufacturer bent on improving its image tried to get people to pronounce it "sexy.")

Several other standards exist for controller-to-drive communication. What's important is that both your drive and controller speak the same language.

The SCSI standard is both more reliable in some ways, and rich enough to control a wide range of devices (including CD-ROM drives and scanners), rather than needing a special sort of controller for each different device type.

USING 5.25-INCH FLOPPY DISKS

The big black square floppy disk (or diskette) is getting rarer these days, but they used to be the only type of PC disk available.

These come in two varieties: double density, and high density. Double density disks store up to 360K and can be read on any 5.25-inch drive. High density disks can store up to 1.2 megabytes and can be read by any high density drive (which most of the ones still in use are).

The only physical difference between the densities of disk is that the magnetic coating is more refined on the high density. A high density disk can actually be formatted and used in a double density drive but then they will hold only as much as a double density disk.

On the outside is a black jacket.

The inside of the jacket is lined with soft fabric that serves to keep the disk clean and moving smoothly.

The disk is made of a thin, flexible plastic called Mylar. Both sides of the disk are coated with iron oxide, the main component of rust.

The disk drive accesses the disk through these slots on both sides of the disk. Don't touch the exposed magnetic surface, as finger grease and grit can damage the delicate disk.

Stress relief notches let the disk have some give in situations where it might get bent.

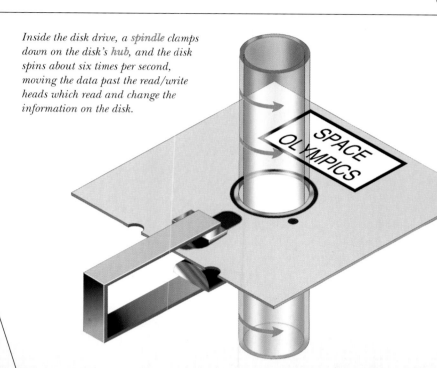

Inside the disk drive, a spindle clamps down on the disk's hub, and the disk spins about six times per second, moving the data past the read/write heads which read and change the information on the disk.

SPACE OLYMPICS

FACTS

Warning: Because the information is stored as magnetic polarity, you can accidentally wipe out information and make a disk unreadable by exposing it to a magnet. Keep your disks far away from magnets!

To be safe, you also should keep it from getting bent and away from grit, grime, heat, liquids, and disk-eating cats.

The write enable notch cut out of the disk lets the drive know that it is okay to write information on the disk. Cover the notch up, and the system will read information from the disk but not write to it, thus protecting the contents of the disk.

A single index hole in the disk is used to help the computer know where on the spinning disk to start reading data.

Music fans will recognize much of how a disk works.

The heads read information by detecting the magnetic status of the little bits of iron oxide on the disk. They write information by putting out a quick magnetic pulse which changes the magnetic status of the iron oxide. This is exactly how an audio cassette (or a VCR, for that matter) works.

A stepper motor moves the heads inward or outward along the spinning disk, to pick up different tracks of information, like the different tracks on a CD or grooves on an LP record.

USING 3.5-INCH FLOPPY DISKS

The little 3.5-inch floppy disk may look like the 5.25-inch disk's kid brother, but if so, he's not only younger and smaller, but tougher and smarter as well.

The well-protected disk stores anywhere from 720K for the double density disks (which define the low end), through the 1.44 megabyte high density disks that most new machines can read and write, up to the extended density 2.88 megabyte disks that are starting to be supported in advanced machines.

This hole indicates a high density disk. Double density disks don't have the hole.

The case is made of a rigid plastic. This disk isn't made to survive *bending, it's made to* avoid *bending. Just because it's in a hard case, don't confuse it with a hard disk!*

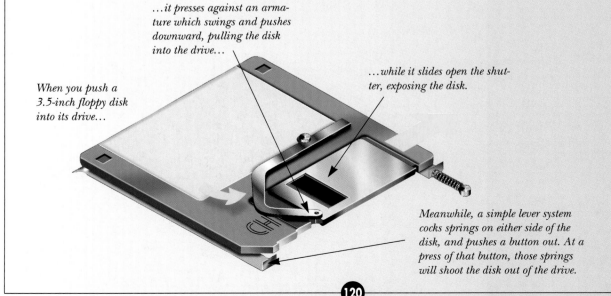

...it presses against an armature which swings and pushes downward, pulling the disk into the drive...

...while it slides open the shutter, exposing the disk.

When you push a 3.5-inch floppy disk into its drive...

Meanwhile, a simple lever system cocks springs on either side of the disk, and pushes a button out. At a press of that button, those springs will shoot the disk out of the drive.

This plastic write protect switch on the back of the disk can be used to cover or reveal the hole in the disk.

Information can be written to the disk only when the hole is covered.

The metal hub helps protect the disk's rigidity better than the hollow center of the larger disk.

This spring-loaded metal shutter protects the magnetic disk from dirt and scratches, and then slides away when the disk is inserted in the machine.

A light emitting diode (LED) shines on the upper right corner of the disk. If a photoreceptor on the other side detects the light passing through, it knows this disk is write-protected, and the drive can then only read the disk and not write to it. Some drives detect the hole using a physical switch instead of an LED.

USING HARD DRIVES

The hard drive is the powerhouse of long-term data storage. It's fast and powerful. When they were originally launched, their five to 10 megabyte storage capacity seemed vast. Now, you would be hard-pressed to find a new hard drive smaller than 40 megabytes. Most people buy hard drives that store hundreds of megabytes, and some store gigabytes (a gigabyte is 1,024 megabytes).

The hard disk drive has multiple platters. The exact number of platters varies from drive to drive, but both sides of all of the platters are always used. Each is made of an aluminum alloy or a ceramic material, which is what makes the hard disk hard. The platter is coated with magnetic material far more sensitive than that on a floppy disk.

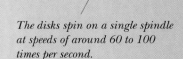

The disks spin on a single spindle at speeds of around 60 to 100 times per second.

The hard disk can spin faster than the floppy because the head never actually touches the disk. Instead, it flies over (or under) the disk at a low height, able to detect and alter the magnetic status on the disk without actually touching it.

Read/write heads

The head actuator moves the read/write heads back and forth across the platters in unison. Only one head is actually in use at a given time.

FACTS

Access time is how long a drive takes to move the disk heads into position to read a requested piece of information. This time is measured in milliseconds, or thousandths of a second. The smaller the access time is, the faster the hard disk operates. Most disks sold these days run between 10 and 20 milliseconds.

Because hard disks are so delicate, they should be protected from vibration or sudden impact, particularly while the computer is on and the disk is running.

Hard drives are sometimes called fixed disks, because the platters are fixed in place and not designed to be taken out of the drive. Some manufacturers now make removable hard disks; they generally involve sealed cartridges containing not only the platters, but also the read/write heads and other parts of the mechanism.

Because they are so delicate, the platters and head mechanism are sealed in an airtight chamber.

TAPE DRIVES

Magnetic tape cartridges for PCs fill a very important niche—they store a lot of information in a removable form. Hundreds, sometimes thousands, of megabytes can be stored on a single tape.

Because files are spread all acorss a long tape, there is no way of getting to any individual piece of information. As such, while they can store a lot of information cheaply, tape drives aren't very good for day-to-day storage use.

They are, however, excellent for making backup copies of information stored elsewhere in case something goes wrong (if, for example, a disk gets damaged or a file is accidentally, irretrievably deleted). The entire contents of a hard drive can fit on a single cartridge.

The basics of a cartridge tape are simple, much like an audio tape. The tape (iron oxide on a ribbon of mylar plastic) goes between two reels inside the cartridge. A tape head reads and writes the information magnetically.

There are a number of different types of tape systems available, using different types of cartridges and different sizes of tapes.

Some store the information in a single line on a tape; then, when they hit the end of the tape, switch direction and move to another line. This way, dozens of tracks can be recorded on a single tape.

FACTS

The earliest IBM PCs sometimes used a cassette tape drive as their primary storage medium. Floppy disk drives were an option costing hundreds of dollars, and it was a long time before a hard drive was an assumed part of a basic PC setup. These early cassette drives used standard audio cassettes, which were far slower and less precise than the high-speed, high-precision specialty cassettes used to back up hard drives these days.

Spinning read/write head automatically checks each bit immediately after writing it

Others store information in diagonal lines across the tape. This allows information to be stored quicker, because the tape doesn't have to move as much when the bits are grouped across the width of the tape.

CD-ROM

The CD in CD-ROM stands for *compact disc*; they are exactly like audio CDs, and many computer CD-ROM drives can be used to play audio CDs. The ROM stands for *read-only memory*, because your computer can only read information from the CD-ROM; it cannot save information on a CD-ROM.

CD-ROMs are used to distribute large programs and vast amounts of information. A CD-ROM disk holds more than 600 megabytes. This makes possible applications that were previously impractical. Entire encyclopedias are available on a single CD-ROM, as are large libraries of programs, and of art.

Information is coded on a series of pits bumps (or *lands*) that spiral out from center of the disc. These pits are so sma and narrow that the spiral goes aroun tens of thousands of times.

Plastic coating

Aluminum

The data on the disc is read from the bottom. The labeling information is on the top, where it will not block the light from reflecting off the data.

REVENGE OF THE MARTIANS

FROM VENUS

COPYRIGHT 1994 MSB INC.

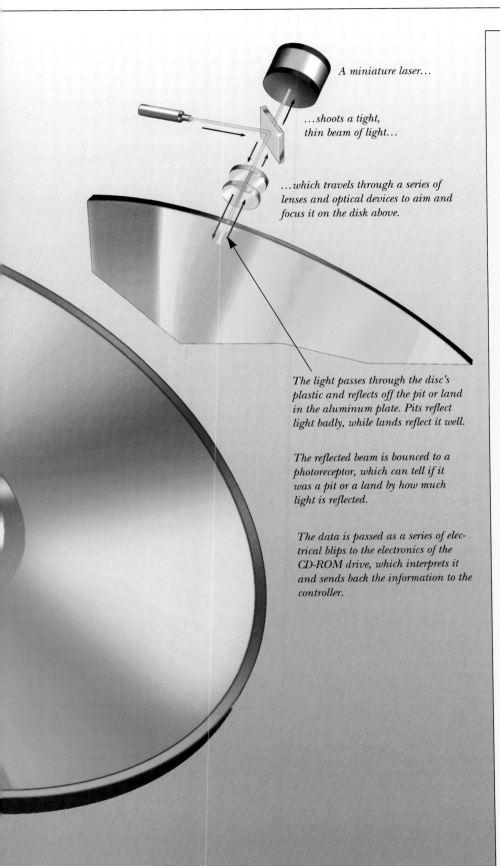

A miniature laser…

…shoots a tight, thin beam of light…

…which travels through a series of lenses and optical devices to aim and focus it on the disk above.

The light passes through the disc's plastic and reflects off the pit or land in the aluminum plate. Pits reflect light badly, while lands reflect it well.

The reflected beam is bounced to a photoreceptor, which can tell if it was a pit or a land by how much light is reflected.

The data is passed as a series of electrical blips to the electronics of the CD-ROM drive, which interprets it and sends back the information to the controller.

FACTS

CD-ROMs are very reliable. The data is physically fixed in place, so it can't get messed up the way magnetic media can. So long as you keep the bottom surface of a CD from getting scratched, it should keep the data safe for decades.

CD-ROMs spin at a variable rate. The motor spins the disc at more revolutions per second when reading data near the center than reading data at the edge. This lets it read the pits at the same rate no matter what part of the disc is being read.

While there is rarely need to play music faster, there is always a need to try to read data faster, so CD-ROM manufacturers have come up with double-, triple-, and even quad-spin CD-ROMs, which can read the CD two, three, and even four times as fast.

Spin rate is not the only speed factor. Access time, the amount of time it takes to find where a given file starts on the disk, makes a major difference in how long you have to wait for your information. Even the fastest CD-ROM drives today take more than 20 times as long to find the start of a string of data as a fast hard drive does.

Multisession CD-ROM drives can read CDs of a special format that can be updated.

OPTICAL DISKS

CD-ROMs show that lasers can be used to read information very precisely, making storage of large amounts of information possible. Unfortunately, CD-ROM drives can only read information, and cannot store it.

Drive manufacturers have created a number of types of disk drives that use a laser to both read and write information, which are all referred to as optical drives. These drives can hold large amounts of information on removable disks, but they all have significant limitations as well. However, they may be the direction for the future of mass storage.

One type of optical disk uses the laser to actually burn pits into the disk, which are then read in the same way that CD-ROMs are read. Once a pit is burned into a disk, there is no way to unburn it, so you can never erase or write over information. It's there forever, and all you can do is read it. Because of this, these disks have the odd name of WORM disks (WORM stands for write once/read mostly).

Magneto-optical (M-O) drives take advantage of the scientific relationship between heat, magnetism, and light to store a lot of information, using both laser and magnetic heads. Information is stored magnetically, but using a metal substance that holds onto its polarity tightly. Heat will encourage any magnetic substance to change its polarity. When writing to a disk, the M-O drive has to let the disk spin by the heads twice. On the first spin, the laser puts out a strong beam of light. This heats up all the magnetic bits, allowing the magnetic head to set them to zero.

A *floptical drive* is like a floppy disk drive, reading and writing data magnetically. More data is fit on the disk by making the tracks of data much thinner. The laser acts like a car headlight, finding the specially etched lines that separate the tracks of data, and checking to make sure the head stays in the right track, which allows data to be used more precisely and much more data to be fit on the disk.

FACTS

The biggest drawback of all of these systems is expense. Floptical drives are the cheapest of the three, available in the $500 range. They also hold the least; the typical floptical system stores about 20 megabytes on a $20 floptical disk. Magneto-optical and WORM drives are available that will store up to a gigabyte of information, but the drives cost around $3,000 and the disks themselves are expensive, generally in the $50 to $250 range.

There aren't standards for some types of optical disks, so you can't just take an optical disk out of one drive and put it into another. A disk might only work with drives from the manufacturer who designed it. (Magneto-optical disks are the exception; a standard for single-sided M-O disks that store 128MB has taken hold, and a double-sided 256MB standard is emerging.)

Because of these limitations, optical disks are nowhere near as prevalent as their magnetic cousins.

On the second spin, the laser heats up just the bits that are to be set to one, and the magnetic head changes only those bits.

Light is made up of vibrations, and magnets have the ability to change the direction that the wave is vibrating. To read the disk, the laser bounces a weak beam of light off of the stored bit. If the reflected light is vibrating one way, the system knows it's a 1, and another way, it's a 0.

RAM DISKS

A RAM disk is sometimes called a *virtual disk* because it's virtually a disk, but there is no disk. In fact, there's no hardware at all! Instead, the RAM disk is a program that takes up a portion of the computer's memory and makes the system pretend that it's a disk.

The program that handles this is a device driver, usually called RAMDRIVE.SYS or VDISK.SYS, and is loaded into your system at startup, as dictated by a command in your CONFIG.SYS file.

Anytime a program allows for a specific drive to be picked, the RAM disk can be picked just like any other disk. The program will pass commands to the operating system to read and write to that disk.

MEMORY

ALLOCATION INFO
DIRECT DRIVE
FILES

The section of RAM is organized much like a normal disk. It has an allocation table to track what files are in what parts of memory, and it can have directories and subdirectories, just like a regular disk.

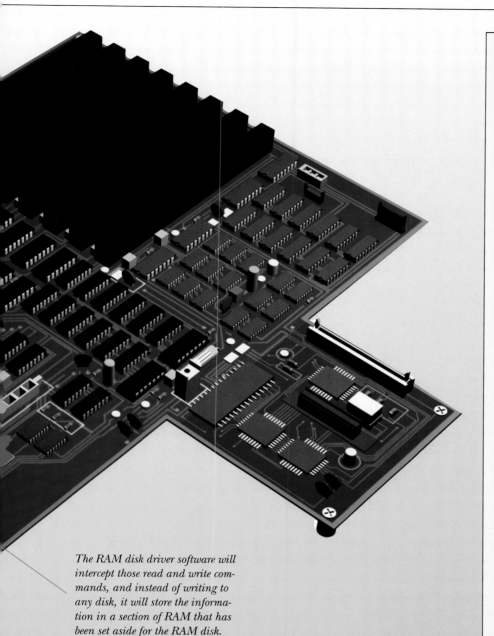

The RAM disk driver software will intercept those read and write commands, and instead of writing to any disk, it will store the information in a section of RAM that has been set aside for the RAM disk.

FACTS

The main advantage of a RAM disk is speed. Because RAM works much faster than physical disk drives, it can speed up operations that involve repeatedly working with the same file.

The main disadvantage of a RAM disk is that it is temporary. Remember, RAM gets cleared when you turn your computer off, so if you have anything in a RAM disk that you want to keep, copy it to a real disk before you're done.

Another disadvantage is that a RAM disk reduces the amount of memory you have available for everything else. RAM disks take up memory even when you haven't put anything in them.

Because a RAM disk counts on you using the operating system to read from and write to a disk, programs that "cheat" around the operating system may not be able to work with a RAM disk. However, most of those programs aren't ones that you'd want to run on a RAM disk anyway (there's really no reason to run a defragmentation program on a RAM disk, for example, since RAM disks don't slow down with fragmentation).

9

WHAT HAPPENS WHEN YOU FORMAT A DISK?

Formatting Floppy Disks

Formatting Hard Disks

WHAT HAPPENS WHEN YOU FORMAT A DISK?

A disk starts out very unstructured, just a lot of little bits of magnetic stuff without any organization, rhyme, or reason. Before the system can start writing files to it, the disk must have a structure—a gridwork into which the information can be placed.

Formatting **a disk is the process of putting the gridwork on the disk and building the organizational structure so that files can be found. Once a disk is formatted, it's ready for the system to write data to it.**

Each platter of a hard disk has two sides.

Side 0
Side 1
Side 2
Side 3
Side 4
Side 5

Even when just manufactured, the disk is clearly made of separate sides, the top and bottom of the physical disk. Each side is referred to by a number.

High level formatting (or soft formatting) is putting down the information and indexes that the operating system needs to keep track of where the files are in the sectors.

BACKUP FAT

BOOT PROGRAM

ROOT DIRECTORY

FAT

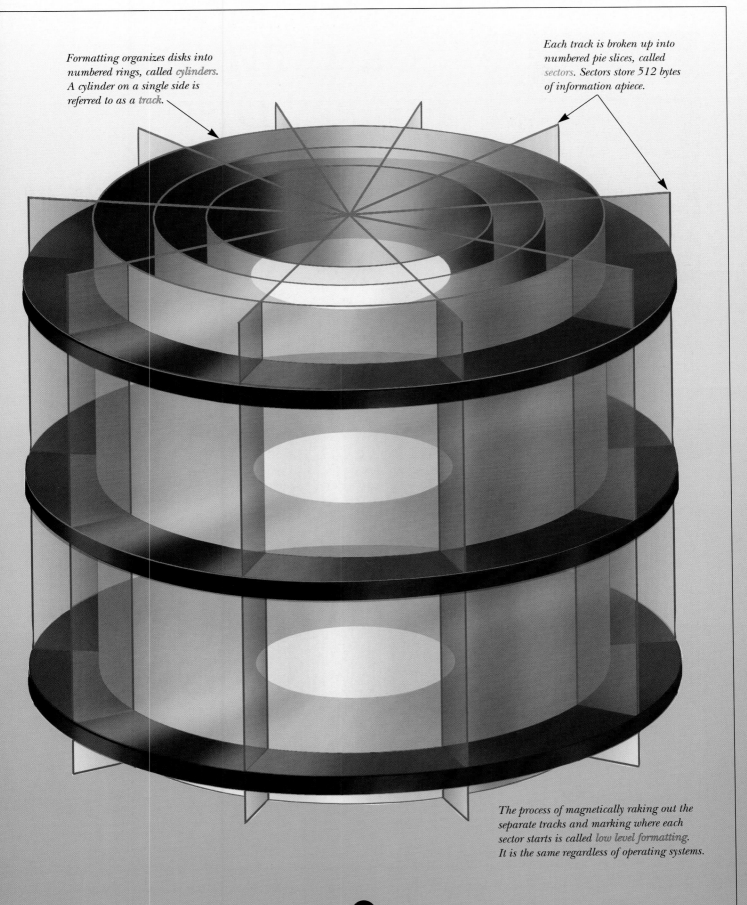

Formatting organizes disks into numbered rings, called cylinders. A cylinder on a single side is referred to as a track.

Each track is broken up into numbered pie slices, called sectors. Sectors store 512 bytes of information apiece.

The process of magnetically raking out the separate tracks and marking where each sector starts is called low level formatting. It is the same regardless of operating systems.

You can buy floppy disks that are already formatted. These cost a little more, but the extra dime is often worth the time saved by not having to format the disk yourself.

Even if you buy your disks unformatted, format them all at once. That way, you won't find yourself in the middle of running a program that needs an empty, formatted floppy disk while all you have is unformatted ones.

Formatting a disk is simple. Just put the unformatted disk into the floppy drive and give the computer the format command. The computer handles all the tricky stuff.

FORMATTING FLOPPY DISKS

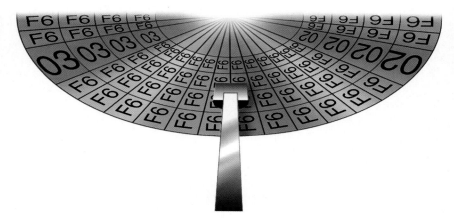

During formatting, the disk marks out each track, starting each sector in the track with a *sector header* showing which sector number it is (as a magnetic bit pattern, of course). It also fills each sector with the hexadecimal value F6.

The number of sectors and tracks depends on the storage capacity of the disk. High density 3.5-inch disks, for example, break 80 tracks on each side of the disk into 18 sectors apiece. Therefore, you get the formula 2 (sides per disk) × 80 (tracks per side) × 18 (sectors per track) × 512 (bytes per sector), which equals 1,440 kilobytes per disk.

One bad piece of data causes the whole sector to be marked as unusable.

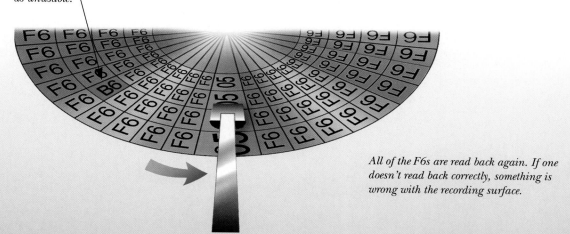

All of the F6s are read back again. If one doesn't read back correctly, something is wrong with the recording surface.

FACTS

Be careful! When you give the command to format a disk, the computer never checks to see if a disk was already formatted. Formatting will wipe out any files that are already stored on the disk.

Of course, that also can work for you. If you have a disk filled with files that you don't need, reformatting will get rid of them quite nicely, leaving you with an empty disk.

Newer versions of the operating system have a command specifically designed for wiping out all of the files on an already formatted disk. When you quick format a disk, it doesn't really reformat the disk at all. Instead, it just clears out the FAT tables and the root directory, so that the disk no longer has any record of having files on it.

The boot program goes on the first sector of the disk (side 0, track 0, sector 1).

The other important structures are set up starting with side 0, track 0, sector 2.

If you use the option to format a system disk, some important operating system files will be put on the floppy. When it is turned on, the computer can get the operating system program from that disk. (The names of the files depend on the version of the operating system.)

BOOT PROGRAM

FAT

BACKUP
FAT

ROOT
DIRECTORY

IO.SYS

MSDOS.SYS

COMMAND.COM

FORMATTING HARD DISKS

Hard disks are low level formatted at the factory. While it is possible to low level format a hard disk again, you probably will never have to. Generally, when we talk about formatting a hard disk, we're only talking about high level formatting.

If you buy a new computer with a hard drive built in, odds are that the manufacturer or dealer already have formatted the disk, and installed the software that you are going to need. But if you buy a hard drive to install in your machine, you will have to format it yourself.

Different operating systems have different ways of organizing files, so each does high level formatting differently. If you want to use and store more than one operating system on a disk, you need to break the disk into partitions.

These are complete cylinders, taking up the same slice of both sides of every platter.

Hard disks generally have anywhere from two to eight platters, and have any number of hundreds of tracks. They almost always have 17 sectors, though.

Each partition is made up of a group of cylinders which act as a separate disk.

The formatting program for each operating system puts the boot program and the other elements of the file system into that partition.

The first partition has two boot programs. The first boot program knows where each partition starts, and which partition has the operating system that the user now wants to run. When this program is run, it loads the boot program of that operating system. The second boot block holds the boot program for the first partition's operating system.

FACTS

Seventeen sounds like a strange number of sectors to have. It's not one of those powers of two that computers love. It is a prime number, evenly divisible only by 1 and itself.

In older PCs, the hard drive would read a sector, and the next sector might be passing under the read/write head before the data from the first sector would be digested. Because the system wasn't ready for the data, it would skip over the sector and wait until the disk spun around again before reading it.

To combat this, interleaving was used. Instead of putting information on consecutive sectors, the drive would use a sector, and then skip some, then use another, then skip some. So with an interleave factor of 2:1 , the drive read (or wrote) the odd-numbered sectors through the 17th sector on a single spin of the disk. After reading the 17th, it skipped the next one (the first again, still on the same track), and read the 2nd, 4th, 6th, etc, until every sector on the track was used.

If disks had a non-prime number of sectors, there'd be problems. Consider a disk with six sectors and a 2:1 interleave factor. It reads the 1st, 3rd, and 5th sectors, skips the 6th, and goes back to the 1st again, never getting to the 2nd, 4th, and 6th!

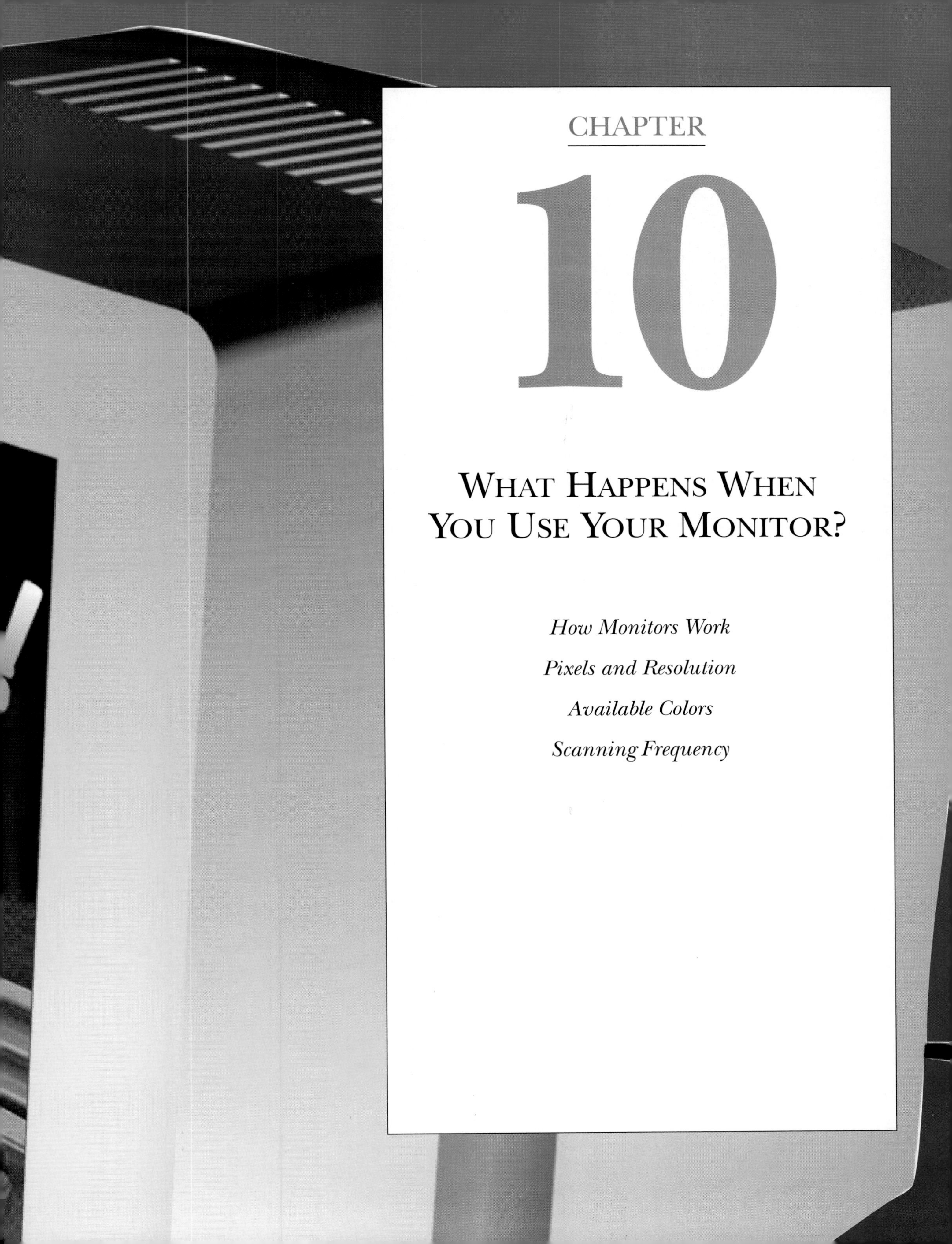

10

WHAT HAPPENS WHEN YOU USE YOUR MONITOR?

How Monitors Work

Pixels and Resolution

Available Colors

Scanning Frequency

WHAT HAPPENS WHEN YOU USE YOUR MONITOR?

The monitor (also called a video display unit or VDU) is the television-like screen that the computer uses to communicate to you.

Early PCs generally used video systems that allowed them only to display letters and other fixed characters, and only in two colors (black and one other color, generally green). Modern PCs support both letters and pictures, in rich color.

Many new PCs have a video adapter built onto the motherboard. Even if it has a video controller built in, many people turn off that controller and use a better controller board.

4 *The monitor turns the pulses into the displayed video image.*

FACTS

New types of video controllers come out frequently. Newer ones handle a more detailed image than the ones they are designed to replace. Traditionally, these have been described by the IBM video standards that they were designed to meet: CGA (Color Graphics Adapter), EGA (Enhanced Graphics Adapter), VGA (Video Graphics Array), and XGA (Extended Graphics Array), in increasing order of quality. These days, most new cards are Super VGA, which means they can do everything that the VGA standard requires, plus handle an even more detailed image. Just how detailed they get varies from card to card.

Other new controllers are better by being faster—that is, able to turn a program request for a changed picture into a displayed picture faster. Some of these are local bus adapters, which can get the image from video RAM over the local bus instead of the slower system bus. Others are graphic accelerators, which lets the CPU use a shorthand method of describing the image, while the card takes care of turning that shorthand into a full image. (You can even get local bus graphic accelerators, which do both!)

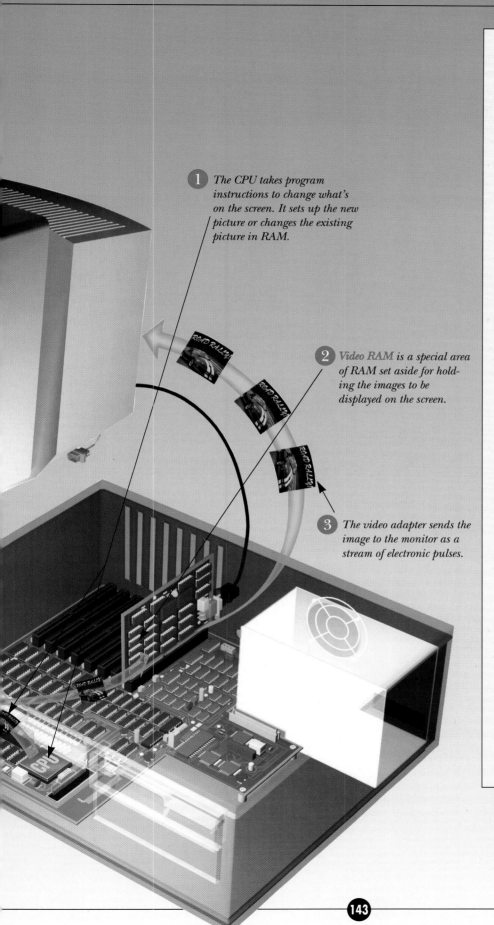

1 *The CPU takes program instructions to change what's on the screen. It sets up the new picture or changes the existing picture in RAM.*

2 *Video RAM is a special area of RAM set aside for holding the images to be displayed on the screen.*

3 *The video adapter sends the image to the monitor as a stream of electronic pulses.*

HOW MONITORS WORK

The standard computer monitor is an outgrowth of television technology, and works much the same way. While there have been and continue to be refinements, the basics are still the same.

Other types of monitors have been developed, but are used mostly for special purposes, ranging from compact liquid crystal displays (LCD) for laptops, to projection systems that put the screen image onto a movie screen for large demonstrations.

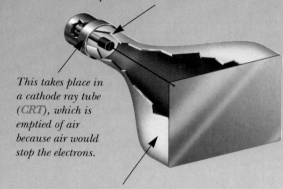

A cathode shoots out a line of varying amounts of subatomic particles called electrons.

This takes place in a cathode ray tube (CRT), which is emptied of air because air would stop the electrons.

Monochrome monitors work like this.

Voltage running through metal plates around the tube causes the electron stream to bend and hit different places on the front of the tube.

The inside of the glass front of the tube is painted with phosphorous. Phosphorous generally looks dark, but when electrons hit it, it becomes excited (to use the technical term) and starts to glow.

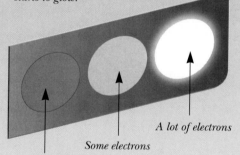

A lot of electrons

Some electrons

No electrons

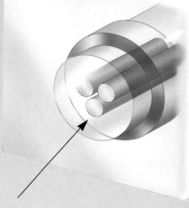

A color monitor is similar, but with three cathodes, all shooting streams of electrons in the same direction.

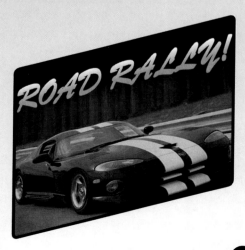

ROAD RALLY!

By hitting different parts of the phosphorous paint with different amounts of electrons, the monitor causes different amounts of glow that look like a picture.

The inside of the tube is painted with dots of three colors of phosphorous: red, green, and blue.

The *shadow mask* makes the beams from one cathode hit only the red dots, another only the green dots, and the third only the blue dots.

Effectively, one cathode is painting a red picture, one a green picture, and one a blue picture. These pictures overlap (because you can make any color out of mixing red, green, and blue light), so it looks like a single, full-color picture.

FACTS

Think about this section the next time you adjust the picture on your TV, and you will really see how the electron beams and phosphorous affect the picture.

Adjusting the *brightness* on your television set changes how many electrons all of the electrons shoot. The more electrons they shoot, the brighter your picture.

Adjusting the *tint* in one direction increases the number of electrons the cathode for the red dots shoots, and decreases the electrons for the green, causing the picture to look redder because the red dots are glowing brighter. In the other direction, it increases the green, and decreases the red.

If you look really closely at the white part of a TV picture, you may actually be able to see the separate red, green, and blue bits.

145

PIXELS AND RESOLUTION

A s was described in Chapter 1, "What Is a Computer?," the computer treats the picture as a gridwork of little rectangles, each with its own color. Each of these little rectangles is a pixel.

200 pixels vertically ——

Monitor resolution is sometimes described in dot pitch (the distance from one pixel to the next), instead of the total numbers of horizontal and vertical pixels.

Each pixel is the smallest unit of the monitor picture, and it has a red phosphorous dot, a green phosphorous dot, and a blue phosphorous dot.

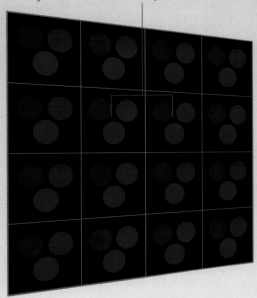

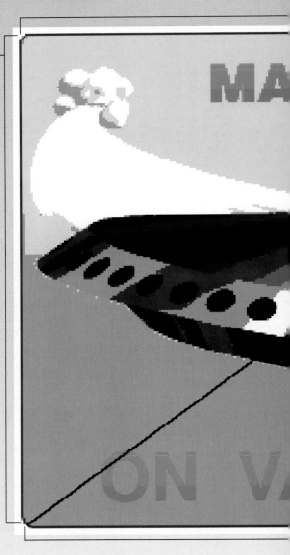

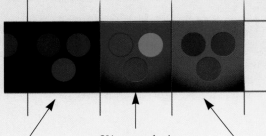

Each pixel can be a different color. If no electrons are shot at the phosphorous dots, it's black.

If just one dot is excited then the pixel will be that color. Even when glowing dimly, the phosphorous is bright enough to look like it is taking up the whole square

To get colors besides red, green, and blue, multiple dots are excited. Their glows seem to mix together.

The resolution of the picture is how detailed the computer displays the image. Resolution is measured as the number of pixels across by the number of pixels down. Above we see the upper left portion of a picture with a 320 by 200 resolution. In the lower right, we see the same picture with a 640 by 400 resolution. Despite the fact that both pictures use the same limited set of colors, the higher resolution picture looks much sharper.

The computer uses different screen modes, with different resolutions and different numbers of colors. What screen modes the computer uses depends on the type of graphics adapter.

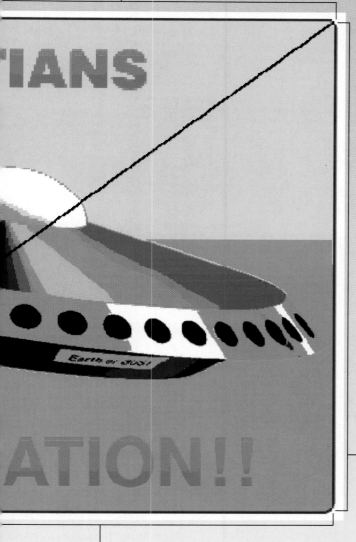

320 pixels horizontally

640 pixels horizontally

400 pixels vertically

FACTS

While there's no problem showing a low resolution picture on a high resolution monitor, the reverse is not true. If you try to show a high resolution picture on a low resolution monitor, it will look fuzzy, if it appears at all. There will be picture pixels that aren't represented anywhere. A higher resolution monitor is always better.

If they don't actually tell you the pixel resolution of the monitor, it can be tough to figure out. The dot pitch will tell you how far apart the dots are, but that doesn't tell you how wide the screen is. They also will give you the screen size, but that won't be how big the screen is across or up-and-down, but *diagonally.* Plus, they give you the screen size in *inches*, and the dot pitch in decimal fractions of *millimeters.*

As a rule of thumb, if you have a Super VGA graphics adapter, you really want a dot pitch of .28 mm (millimeters) or less; VGA, you should probably go with .31 or less; EGA, .42 or less.

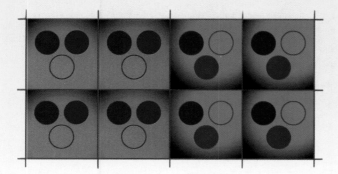

It's no problem if the computer is using an image of lower resolution than the monitor is capable of handling. More than one screen pixel can be used for each of the picture's pixels, so it will still take up the whole screen.

AVAILABLE COLORS

olor adds a lot of richness to using a computer. It's more than just *pretty*; color serves to communicate information very clearly, making certain parts of the screen stand out.

When using spreadsheets, word processing programs, databases, and the like, you really only need a handful of colors. If you are using your computer for artistic programs, or are an avid game player, you probably will want a graphics adapter that can handle a wide range of colors.

The choice of colors for that screen is called its palette. Normal screen modes let you use anywhere from two to 256 colors on screen at a time. (Special, expensive true color adapters allow more than that.) They don't all have to be different. Some programs take advantage of having two palette locations with the same color to perform special display tricks.

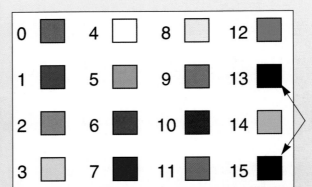

0	4	8	12
1	5	9	13
2	6	10	14
3	7	11	15

The user looking at the picture c... tell the difference between 13 (bla... and 15 (black). The computer ca...

Same screen mode, same picture, different four-color palette.

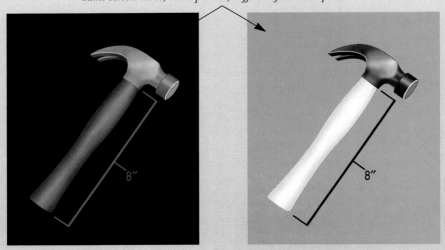

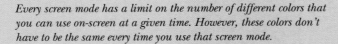

Every screen mode has a limit on the number of different colors that you can use on-screen at a given time. However, these colors don't have to be the same every time you use that screen mode.

If the palette is how many different crayons you have, the **range** is the size of the crayon box. The computer has to represent each possible color as a number, so it can store the palette. On some modes for some adapters, you only have 16 colors to choose your palette from, because the computer only uses four bits to store each color.

No nice candy-apple red.

FACTS

When you have more than 16 million colors, you have more colors than the human eye can distinguish. Even when they are right next to each other, the eye can't quite make out the difference between, say, a dot of red and another dot that is just 1/256th redder, or one that has a smidgen of blue added. Because of this, you probably will never need more than 24 bits of color.

16
OLORS

The more bits used, the more "crayons" you have to choose from. Common adapter modes use 8 bits (256 colors), 16 bits (about 65,000 colors), 18 bits (about 250,000 colors), and, on really high-end adapters, 24 bits (over 16 million colors—a big box of crayons!). The larger ranges break the bits down into sets, each describing how intense one of the primary colors is on the screen pixel.

Six bits of red gives 64 choices...

...+6 bits of green...

...+6 bits of blue...

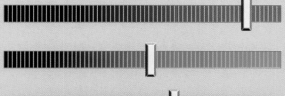

...equals an 18-bit color—the perfect bubble-gum pink!

SCANNING FREQUENCY

When the electrons hit the phosphorous, it starts to glow, but will very quickly fade away. Because of this, the cathodes have to keep repainting the picture on the screen.

It may not sound like the speed at which it repaints the screen would be that important, but it really is, because the monitor has to be able to match the speed at which the adapter keeps sending information to the screen.

The cathode shoots the electrons straight across a line of pixels, and then quickly goes to the start of the next line and shoots that one. It repeats this until it hits the bottom of the screen, and then starts the whole thing again.

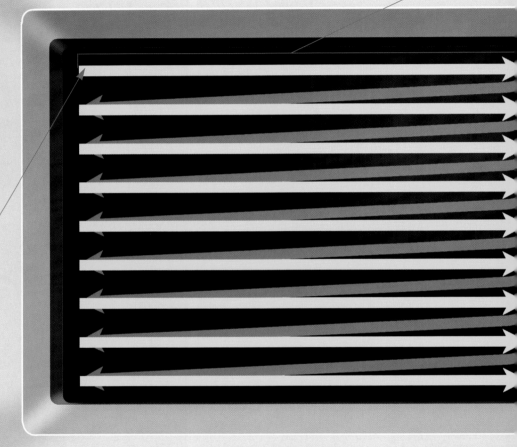

Multiscan monitors handle a range of scanning speeds, so are more likely to be suited to different adapter cards.

The horizontal scanning frequency is how fast the electron beam sweeps across one row of pixels. This is measured in kilohertz (kHz, pronounced "kill-o-hurts"), which means thousands of cycles per second. So a good monitor that has a 40 kHz horizontal frequency can paint 40,000 lines across the screen per second.

The vertical scanning frequency is how fast it takes to paint the whole screen. This is measured in hertz (Hz, pronounced "hurts"), which means cycles per second. So a monitor with a 70 Hz vertical scanning frequency can repaint the whole screen 70 times every second.

Some monitors do something called interlace. First they scan only every other line...

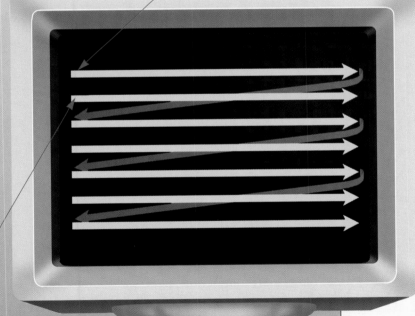

...and then they come back and scan the lines they missed.

FACTS

When setting up your computer, you have to know if your graphics adapter is putting out a digital or an analog signal. A digital signal has the color information encoded as a number, while an analog signal just puts out the red, green, and blue components on separate wires as varying strengths of voltage, showing the monitor how strong to make the electron beam.

Digital may sound like it would be better (it sure sounds more like a computer, coding it as a number), but analog actually makes the better picture. All of the VGA and Super VGA cards use an analog signal.

Most new monitors can only handle an analog signal, although some can handle either. Digital-only monitors are still available. Check before you buy one, so you know that it matches your adapter.

Interlace monitors are cheaper than non-interlace monitors, but the picture will seem to flicker a bit. This can be very tiring on the eyes after a while. (Televisions are interlaced, but because the picture is moving and because it isn't made up of straight lines of color, you don't notice the flicker.)

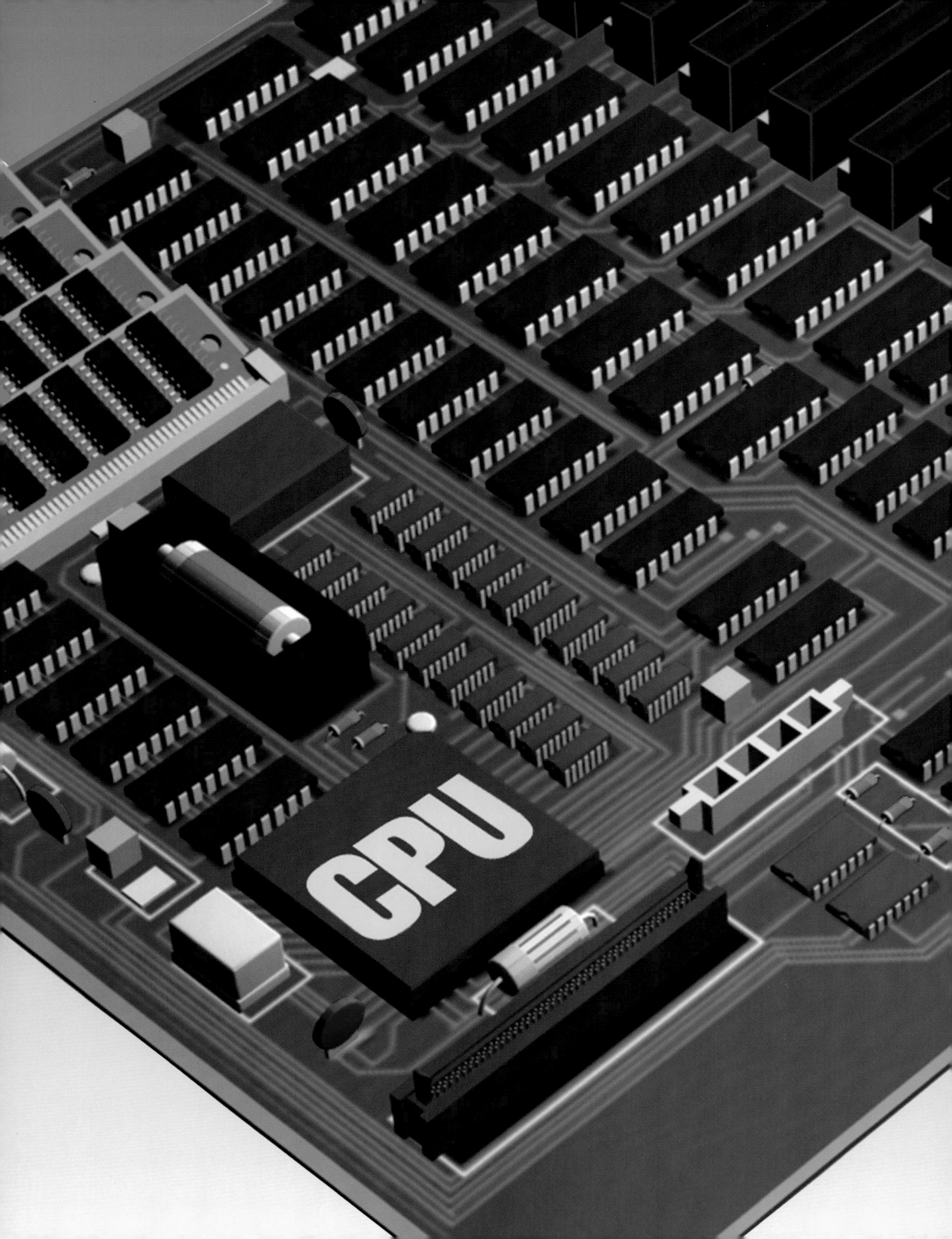
CPU

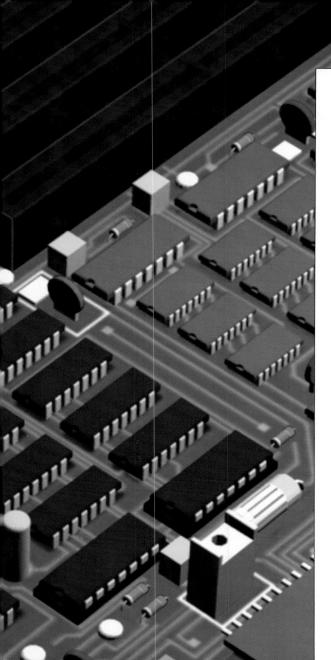

CHAPTER

11

WHAT HAPPENS WHEN YOU USE YOUR I/O PORTS?

Parallel Ports

Serial Ports

WHAT HAPPENS WHEN YOU USE YOUR I/O PORTS?

The computer frequently is attached to devices that aren't actually built into the computer or installed on a board inside. Printers and external modems are clear examples of this.

To provide a way to talk to these devices, the computer has standard I/O ports (input/output ports). These connectors let you attach cables that go to these devices. With standard ports that communicate in standard ways, it is easy to hook a new device up to your computer. You generally don't need to change any of the computer's internal hardware, just plug the device's cable into the computer and set up the software to recognize it. Without these standards, every peripheral would have its own special way of connecting the computer, and attaching new devices to your computer would be much more difficult.

The CPU communicates with the I/O controller via the system bus.

The I/O controller can be a card or it can be built onto the system board. (Some systems have different controllers for different ports.) The controller translates between the set of signals that the system bus uses to communicate and the signals that the port uses to communicate.

The connectors slide a group of pins into a bunch of sockets, connecting the port's wiring to the wires in the cable.

Information is sent over the wires as electrical pulses. At a given time, each wire is on (carrying a voltage) or off (not carrying a voltage).

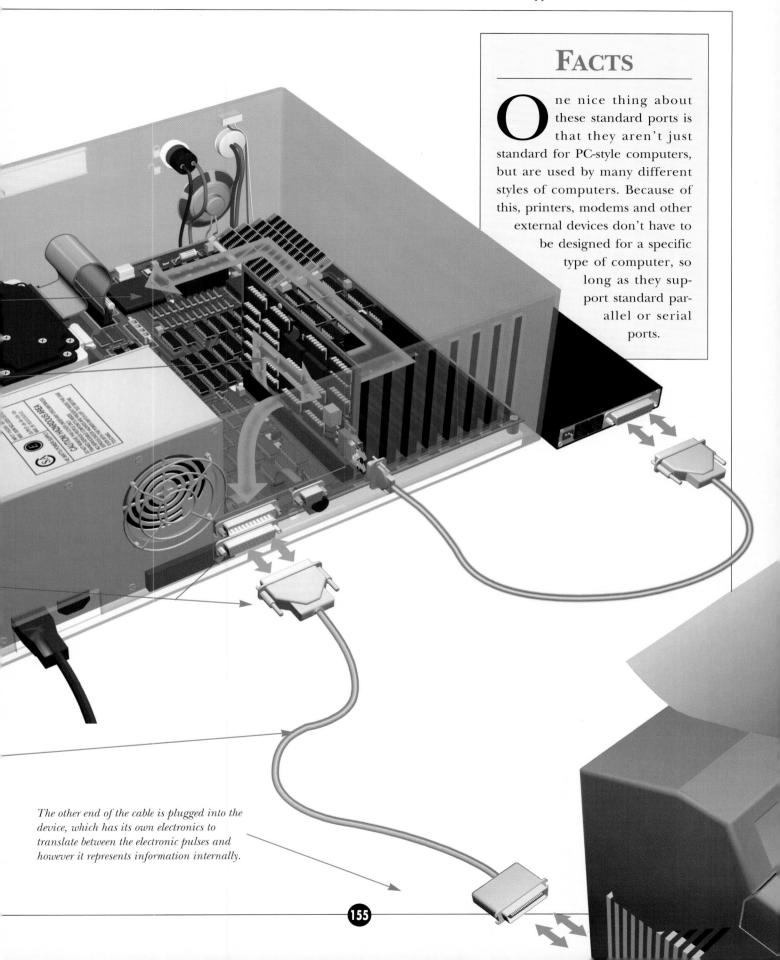

The other end of the cable is plugged into the device, which has its own electronics to translate between the electronic pulses and however it represents information internally.

PARALLEL PORTS

Parallel ports send out data an entire byte at a time, one bit each over eight different wires. Since the bits are moving alongside each other, they're considered to be moving parallel, hence the name.

Most printers hook up to parallel ports. These ports were designed specifically for printers, though they can be used for other things. The device name for the parallel ports (LPT1, LPT2, LPT3, etc.) comes from *Line PrinTer*, which is a fast type of printer that types a whole line at a time. Parallel ports were good for sending to these printers, because they sent a whole byte at a time, instead of just a bit.

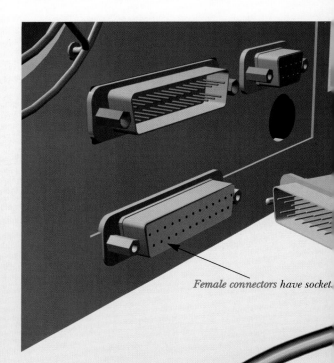

Female connectors have socket.

The *auto feed pin* tells the printer whether to expect separate commands to set the print head back to the beginning of the line and to advance the paper, or if it should automatically advance the paper every time the print head goes back.

The *strobe pin* acts as a metronome, cycling on and off every time a new bit has been sent, so the printer (or other device) knows when to check the line.

The printer uses the *acknowledge line* to indicate when it is ready for more data.

These carry the byte, one bit per line.

The printer uses the *busy line* to tell the computer that it is too busy with the data already sent to accept any more.

This pin is used by the printer to signal when it is out of paper, so it's called *paper out*.

Most printers have a button marked Select, which the user can toggle to take the printer off-line, preventing it from accepting any data from the computer. The *select pin* lets the computer know whether the printer is off-line.

These pins provide electrical grounds.

The *fault pin* is used by the printer to say that something is wrong (but not something announced by another pin, like paper out).

The computer uses the *init pin* to reset the printer, as if it has been turned off and on again. This lets a program clear any special printer settings that the previous program might have set up.

The *select input line* lets the computer take the printer off-line or put it on-line again.

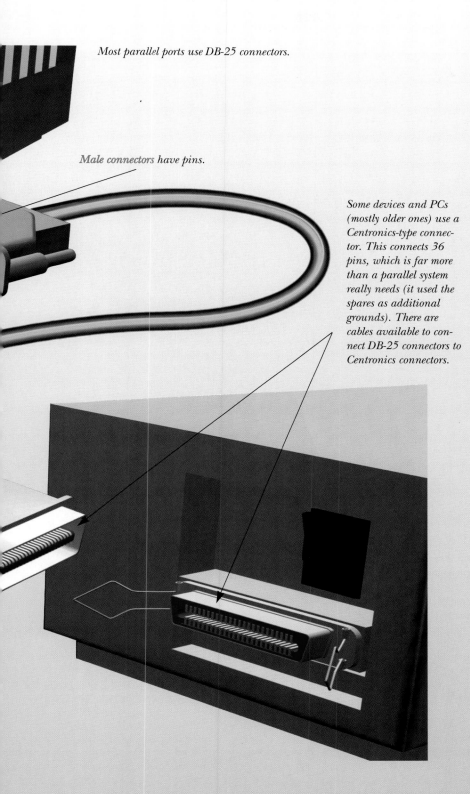

Most parallel ports use DB-25 connectors.

Male connectors have pins.

Some devices and PCs (mostly older ones) use a Centronics-type connector. This connects 36 pins, which is far more than a parallel system really needs (it used the spares as additional grounds). There are cables available to connect DB-25 connectors to Centronics connectors.

FACTS

The parallel port is designed for sending data *from* your PC *to* a device, with the device just communicating its ability to receive data. It also can be used in the other direction. It is very awkward to use to send messages back and forth, though, because it only has wires for one set of data. That's why the parallel port is not used with modems, which depend on two-way communication, and, therefore, use a different type of port.

Because the parallel cable is carrying so many wires of data, there is a real risk of interference. The longer a stretch of cable you use, the more the risk. It's generally not a good idea to put a parallel device more than ten feet from the computer.

Most computers have only one parallel port, because these ports are used by printers only. If you need to hook up more than one device, you can get a controller with another port, or you can get a switch box, which lets you switch between two devices. The switch box will work fine as long as you don't need to use both devices at once.

SERIAL PORTS

The serial port transfers each character as a *series* of bits along a single wire. There are a pair of data wires, so that data can flow in both directions at once. This is why it's used to hook up to external modems. Serial ports also are used for printers and mice.

The device names for serial ports are COM1, COM2, etc. COM stands for *communications*. Most PCs have two, some even more, because there are so many uses.

Connecting one computer directly to another is done by hooking their serial ports together using a null modem cable. This cable flips the transmit line computer into the receive line of the other. It also flips other lines, so that the signals go to the right place.

The current standard for PC serial connections is a DB-9 connector, the DB-25's little brother.

First, an extra bit set to 1 is sent to notify the receiver that a character is about to arrive.

If only ASCII data is being sent, only seven bits need be used.

Just like memory parity, the serial port can be set up to send a parity bit that can be used by the receiving device to check that the bits arrived. There are two ways of calculating parity bits, called odd and even parity. Much rarer are setups where the bit is always set to 1 (mark parity) or always set to 0 (space parity).

| START BIT | 7 OR 8 DATA BITS | PARITY BIT | STOP BITS |

Each character is sent as a series of bits. There are a number of different things that the bit packet can include, and both the sending and receiving device need to be set to include the same things so that they can understand each other. For example, the devices could be configured as 8-N-1 (eight bits of data, no parity bit, one stop bit), or as 7-E-2 (seven bits of data, even parity bit, two stop bits).

One or two more bits set to 1 are sent to make it clear the character is finished.

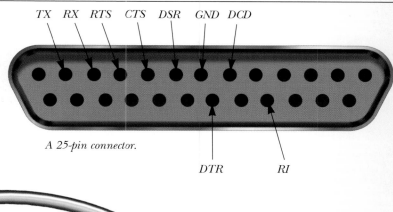

TX RX RTS CTS DSR GND DCD

DTR   RI

A 25-pin connector.

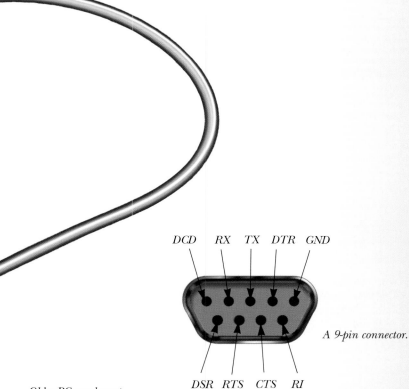

DCD RX TX DTR GND

DSR RTS CTS RI

A 9-pin connector.

Older PCs and most devices use DB-25 connectors. Only nine pins are needed, however.

FACTS

T X is the transmit line that the computer sends out data on.

RX is the receive line for data sent to the computer.

DCD is data carrier detect. It is turned on by modems to indicate that they have hooked up to another modem.

The RTS line is turned on by the computer to send the device a request to send data to the computer; it's the computer's way of letting the device know it is ready.

CTS is clear to send, which is the device's way of letting the computer know it is ready to receive.

DTR (data terminal ready) is a signal turned on by the computer to indicate it is connected and on.

DSR (data set ready) is turned on by the device to indicate it is ready and on.

RI is the ring indicator, set by modems to tell the computer that the phone is ringing.

GND is an electrical ground wire.

Shielded serial cables can safely connect a computer to a device 75 or even 100 feet away.

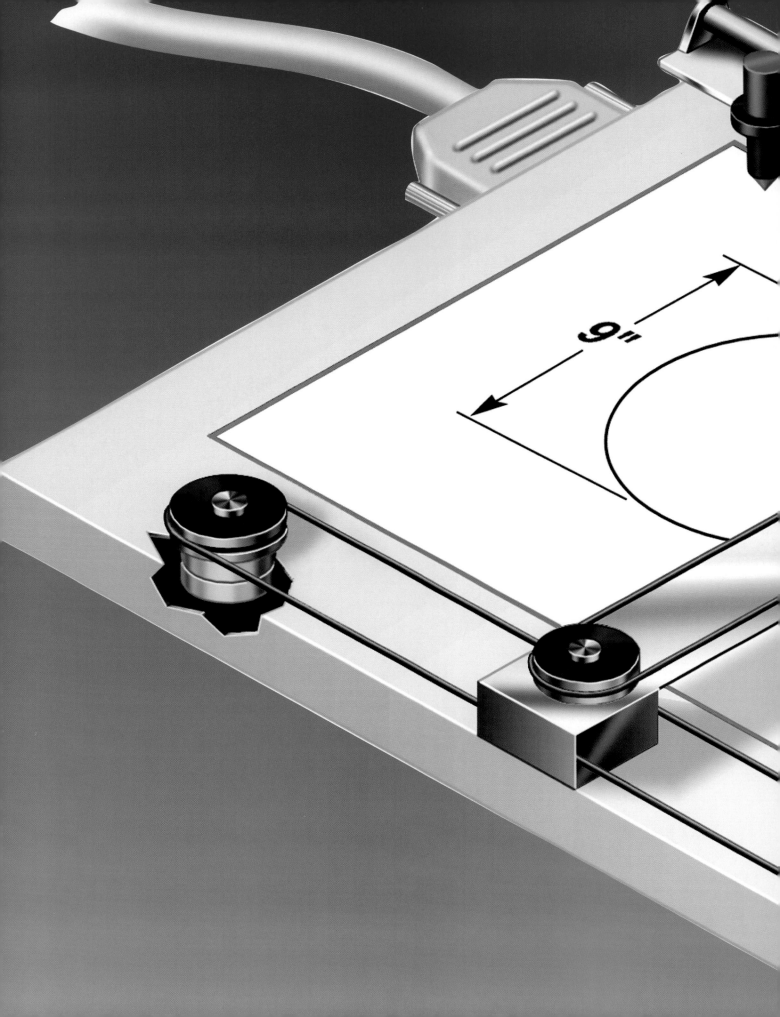

12

WHAT HAPPENS WHEN YOU USE YOUR PRINTER?

WHAT HAPPENS WHEN YOU USE YOUR PRINTER?

Printers take information from the computer and put it on paper. The printing process begins when the computer program sends information to the printer. Sometimes, this is filtered through a special subprogram called a printer driver, which knows the command language for this specific printer. The information (a combination of ASCII text and printer commands) travels over the system bus to the I/O controller. The I/O controller sends the information out through the parallel port (or sometimes the serial port) to the printer.

The type of printer you choose depends on your budget and the type of output you need. If you need to print simple in-house memos or grocery lists, a dot-matrix printer may be sufficient. For newsletters or desktop publishing, on the other hand, a laser printer is more appropriate because of its higher quality.

The printer has its own internal computer which receives the information.

Because the computer can send information far faster than the printer can print it, the printer stores the information in RAM. This storage RAM is called a buffer.

The printer takes information from the buffer and prints it onto paper.

FACTS

By using ASCII character codes combined with the standard keys on your keyboard, you can even produce documents that include pound symbols (£), yen symbols (¥), and other special signs or symbols not available on the keyboard. The printed versions of the symbols will vary depending on the type of printer, available fonts, and print resolution.

To a certain extent, the operating system of the computer can control the printer. You may be able to switch the printer to produce characters from a different language. Consult your operating system manual for specific instructions and cautions.

If the buffer fills up, the printer tells the computer to stop sending information, and then requests more data when the buffer has some space.

DAISYWHEEL PRINTERS

Daisywheel printers print sharp, clean-looking documents, which made them popular for a number of years. They are designed for printing text (which they do very well), but not pictures and graphs (which they don't do at all). The development of other printers which could print sharply but also could print pictures and graphs, seriously hurt the popularity of the daisywheel. Many are still in use, but this printing technology is now out-of-date.

The printer's name comes from the fact that the part which shapes its letters looks like a flower. By replacing this *daisywheel*, the user could change the size and look of the characters (also known as the *font*).

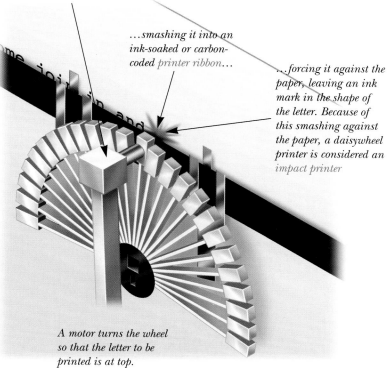

The *hammer pin* hits the letter arm…

…smashing it into an ink-soaked or carbon-coded *printer ribbon*…

…forcing it against the paper, leaving an ink mark in the shape of the letter. Because of this smashing against the paper, a daisywheel printer is considered an *impact printer*

A motor turns the wheel so that the letter to be printed is at top.

A sheet feeder feeds pieces of paper into the printer, one piece at a time. Other daisywheel printers use a *tractor feed* paper feeding setup, where a special continuous chain of paper goes through the printer.

The print head *(the daisy-wheel, motor, and hammer pin) is pulled by wires or a belt along the carriage (a metal rod).*

The paper wraps around a cylinder called the *platen, similar to the cylinder in a typewriter.*

The ribbon is generally a continuous loop that coils inside a replaceable ribbon cartridge.

SELECT

LINE FEED

FORM FEED

The select button lets you take the printer off-line, so it stops printing and stops accepting information from the computer.

A motor advances the paper line by line. The user also can advance the paper, using either a platen knob or the control buttons.

FACTS

While the inability to print graphics was perhaps the biggest problem with daisywheel printers, other factors contributed to its fall from popularity. *Speed* was a big factor—daisywheels are generally the slowest category of printer.

Noise was another problem—from the constant pounding of the hammer against the daisywheel, and that against the page and platen. Many people used special muffling enclosures around their printers. Printer manufacturers found ways of making the printers quieter, but could never make them as quiet as non-impact printers.

Flexibility was another problem. Because the wheel had to be physically changed to get a different font, putting multiple fonts in a single document was impractical. This ruled out not only fancy type mixing, but even simple things like *italics*.

Despite all this, daisywheels still have their niches. They are often considered the best printers for multipart forms, for example, because the letter strikes the paper hard enough to make a clear impression on several layers of paper.

DOT-MATRIX PRINTERS

Remember that the computer thinks of pictures as groups of dots, and it displays words *and* pictures as groups of dots (pixels). Dot-matrix printers print out pictures and words as a grid (or matrix) of dots.

Dot-matrix printers are constructed like their daisywheel cousins. The only part that's drastically different is the print head.

While dot-matrix printers can use sheet feeders, most use a tractor feed mechanism. Tractor-like treads pull a chain of special hole-edged paper through the paper path.

The ribbon cartridge often travels with the print head.

Inside the print head are one or two columns of magnetic metallic pins resting inside wire coils. This coil/pin combination is called a solenoid.

When an electrical charge is applied to the coil, the coil turns into a magnet that repels the magnet of the pin.

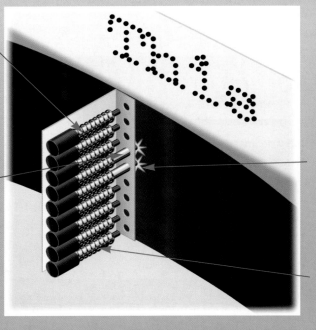

This drives the end of the pin through a hole in the print head, smashing the inked ribbon against the paper. Hence, the dot-matrix also is an impact printer.

When the current is discontinued, the coil loses its magnetism, and the pin returns to its original position.

Tractor-feed paper is available in different sizes and types. All of it is perforated between sheets for easy separation. Most of it is perforated by the holes, so you can tear off the tractor-feed holes and leave a normal-looking piece of paper.

You can often change font size and shape through control buttons on your printer, as well as through program commands.

With 24 pins in the print head, letters and pictures look sharp.

Dot-matrix printers with only 9 pins are cheaper, but because the letters are made up of fewer, larger dots, it doesn't look as good.

This is 24-pin type.

This is 9-pin type.

This is NLQ 9-pin type.

Newer 9-pin printers can take multiple passes on each line, printing more dots. This near letter quality (NLQ) mode is slow and still doesn't look as good as printing with 24 pins.

FACTS

Dot-matrix printers are cheapest in the initial price (prices start at under $150), and tied with daisywheels in being cheapest in per page costs (paper and ribbons). While dot-matrix printers are not as loud as daisywheels, they still have the high-pitched noise of the small pins hitting to make every dot. Dot-matrix printers are faster than daisywheels, but not as fast as laser printers for most jobs.

Some dot-matrix printers can use special rainbow-hued ribbons to print in simple color, using rough dots of four different colors.

Dot-matrix printers often have a number of different fonts (character shapes and sizes) built in. Many also can accept font designs sent from the computer. In some cases, instead of sending the font design to the printer and then sending the text, the computer will send the whole page as a picture, with dot patterns that make up letters in the picture.

Some printers are designed to take the paper up through a slot in the bottom of the printer. By not having to bend the paper around, the chances of the paper getting jammed in the printer are greatly reduced.

INKJET PRINTERS

One big problem with ribbon-based printers is the repeated use of the ribbon. The ribbon cycles repeatedly through the machine, a little of the ink coming off of it every time you print, and the amount of ink delivered with each dot printed starts to lessen and get uneven. Even with a brand new ribbon, the ink saturation tends to be a bit uneven, making rich solid areas of black difficult to achieve.

Inkjet printers address that problem. Instead of using ink-soaked ribbons, they use cartridges filled with liquid ink, which provide an even supply until the cartridge runs low (at which point, it is replaced).

The ink cartridge rests in the print head, which is slid across the page on a carriage.

This figure shows a cutaway version of the inside of an inkjet printer. An advantage of inkjet printing is that it is sheetfed; many printers also have a manual feed mechanism so that you can insert a single sheet of letterhead or other special paper without having to open the printer or switch paper trays.

Most inkjet printers use single sheets of paper taken from a bin in the bottom of the printer. Because cheap paper will make the ink spread and look fuzzy, inkjet printers need good, non-porous paper.

FACTS

Since the ink is just lightly squirted onto the page, rather than hammered into it, inkjets are very quiet printers.

You can get an inkjet printer for about the cost of a good dot-matrix printer, and the inkjet will have better quality output. However, the high costs of ink cartridges and the need for better paper make the per page cost pretty high—about 6 cents per page versus about a penny for a dot-matrix printer.

Many inkjet printers can print in color, using cartridges with three colors of ink. Mixing these colors in a fine dot pattern lets the printer create a wide range of hues. Generally, you would have to go to a more expensive printing process to beat the quality of color of a good color inkjet.

The ink flows into a row of nozzles, which serve the same purpose as the row of pins on a dot-matrix print head. The holes in the nozzles are so small that the surface tension of the ink keeps the ink inside. Heating individual nozzles causes the ink to expand slightly, forming a bubble outside the hole. The bubble of ink hits the page, leaving a small dot. Current inkjets use dots that are a mere 1/300th or even 1/600th of an inch across.

The paper tray of the printer can hold enough paper to prevent constant reloading.

LASER PRINTERS

The laser printer has taken the printer field by storm, offering amazing print quality, high speed, powerful ability to handle graphics, and much quieter operation than the impact printers. Often, the printers cost more than the computers they were attached to, but prices have been plummeting. They are more expensive than other sorts of printers, but the additional cost is often worth it.

Much of the internals of the laser printer are based around concepts originally used in photocopiers. The two machines are very similar; the laser printer is just copying an image from the computer rather than copying a piece of paper.

8 *The powerful laser printer computer has a large bank of RAM, often measured in megabytes. In this RAM, the printer builds a complete image of the page before it starts printing any of it. Thus, laser printers are considered page printers.*

7 *The corona wire dissipates the static charge that is left on the drum, leaving it clear for the next time around.*

6 *The static charge on the paper sucks the toner off the rotating drum, leaving the toner on the page.*

Laser printers use page description languages (PDL), which allow communication of the layout and design of the page, rather than just data, choice of fonts, and dot graphics descriptions that most lower end printers support. A circle, for example, is described not as a series of dots but by a simple command for the laser printer to draw a circle this *big centered at* that *point on the page. Most also allow for type being put down in other than a straight horizontal line.*

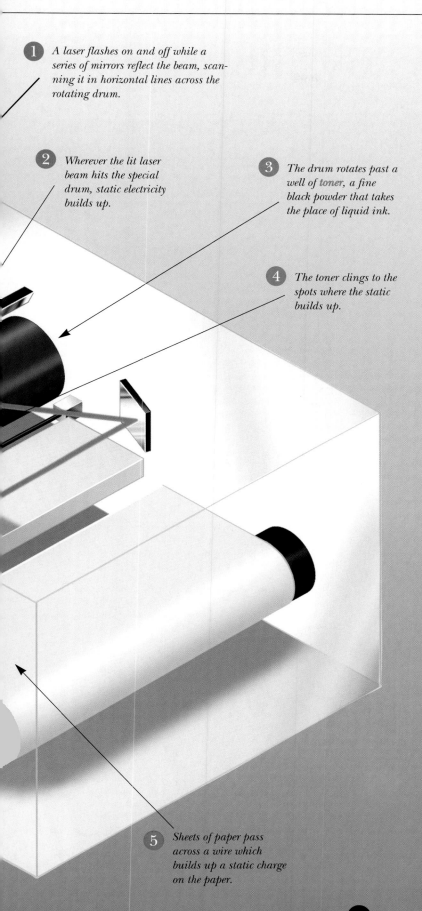

1 *A laser flashes on and off while a series of mirrors reflect the beam, scanning it in horizontal lines across the rotating drum.*

2 *Wherever the lit laser beam hits the special drum, static electricity builds up.*

3 *The drum rotates past a well of toner, a fine black powder that takes the place of liquid ink.*

4 *The toner clings to the spots where the static builds up.*

5 *Sheets of paper pass across a wire which builds up a static charge on the paper.*

FACTS

Laser printer resolution is measured in dots per inch (dpi) of toner on the paper. Horizontal resolution is set by how many times the laser can turn off and on going across the drum. Vertical resolution is set by how thick a line the laser is making with each pass. The horizontal and vertical resolutions don't have to be the same. Both start at 300 dpi and go up from there, with higher resolution printers costing more.

Many newer laser printers use an enhancement technology, which varies the size of the beam on each individual dot. This allows for more even grays and smoother edges on curves.

Laser printer speed is measured in pages per minute (ppm). The speed for a printer, however, is often a best-case estimate. The amount of processing the internal computer has to do varies with the complexity of the page and its use of the page description language.

Laser printers come with a number of fonts built in. Most also can accept new ones stored on the user's computer, or ones stored in ROM cartridges in easily accessed slots.

Per page costs of a laser printer (paper, replaceable toner cartridges, etc.) are higher than for impact printers.

PLOTTERS

The printers we have looked at so far handle lines and curves by turning them all into series of dots. That's fine for most uses, but sometimes you need actual lines and curves. For that, you need a plotter. Plotters draw in much the same way as people do, only a lot more precise. This lets them turn out fine-looking charts and technical drawings, often in color.

A flatbed plotter has a table where the paper rests.

One motor is used to move a crossbar back and forth across the page.

Another motor in the crossbar moves the pen holder up and down along the crossbar.

Moving just the crossbar or just the pen, straight horizontal lines can be made.

Plotters can lift the pen from the paper. Most also can change pens, dropping one into its slot and picking another up from another slot. Different pens not only let it draw lines of different colors, but also of different thicknesses.

The plotters even make its letters up out of a series of lines and curves. This lets it make letters of any size, by changing the lengths of the lines and curves.

The design of the page is received by the plotter as descriptions of lines and curves, and is processed as a set of actions by two motors.

FACTS

Plotter speed is how fast the plotter can draw a line, in inches per second. The amount of time it takes to draw an entire page depends on how many lines are on the page, and how long they are. The amount of time it takes to complete the drawing depends on how many lines, how long they are, and how often the plotter has to change pens.

Plotter sizes are described using the letters that draftsmen use to describe the paper sizes that they use, starting with A as the smallest, and getting larger with each subsequent letter.

Some roller plotters use inkjet technology, spraying the ink on the paper rather than rolling it on.

By varying the speed of the pen's vertical movement and the horizontal movement of crossbar, diagonal lines and curves can be made.

Drafting often requires very large drawings. Rather than making huge flatbeds, larger drawings can be made faster by roller-based plotters.

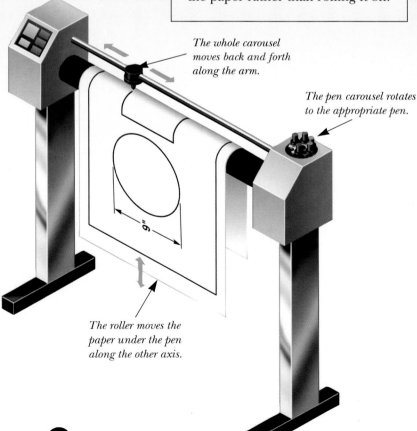

The whole carousel moves back and forth along the arm.

The pen carousel rotates to the appropriate pen.

The roller moves the paper under the pen along the other axis.

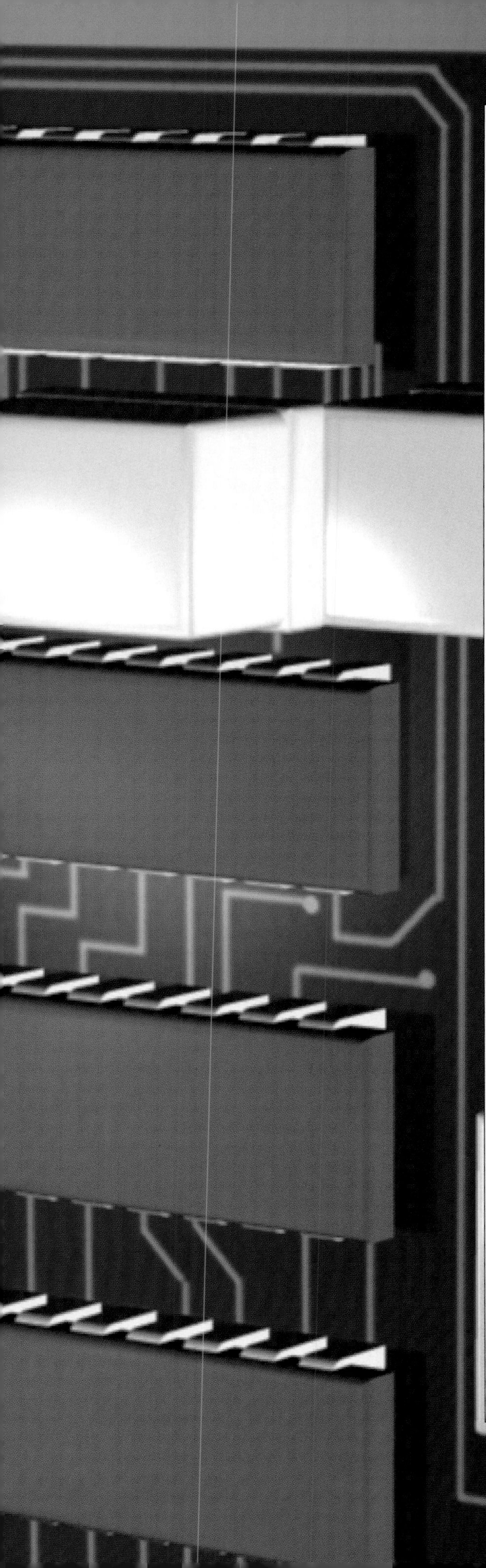

13

WHAT HAPPENS WHEN YOU USE YOUR MODEM?

Types of Modems

Modulation

Transfer Protocols

WHAT HAPPENS WHEN YOU USE YOUR MODEM?

The modem (pronounced "moe-dum") acts as an interface between your computer and a phone line. It allows you to access other computers attached to modems. Anywhere you can reach by phone, your computer may now be able to reach.

By allowing this sort of long distance contact, you cannot only arrange to transfer files between distant computers, but you also have access to a wide range of computer networks, bulletin boards, and other special services.

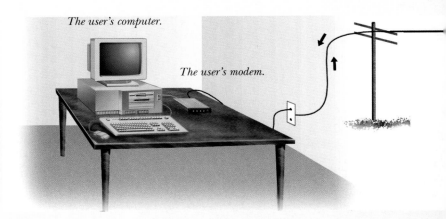

The user's computer.

The user's modem.

1. The user's computer sends a command to the user's modem to dial a phone number.

2. The user's modem dials the number.

3. The remote modem is set up to answer the phone. It sends a whistling sound over the phone line to announce its presence and the speed that it expects to communicate.

4. The user's modem whistles back until they agree on a speed and get in synchronization.

5. The user's computer sends data (including user input) to the modem.

6. The user's modem sends that information over the phone line.

The remote computer.

The remote modem.

FACTS

With all sorts of highly publicized cases of computer crackers (people who break into computers to access data or wreak mischief), many people are scared to attach a modem to their computers. The fear that someone may break into your computer is unfounded, because your computer will not answer the phone line unless you *specifically* set it up to do so. The systems that have cracking problems are those that are designed to allow people access from remote locations —BBS systems, computers at a central office that systems at other offices need to exchange information with, etc.

7. The remote modem turns the phone signal back into the information.

8. The remote computer receives the data, and the program reacts to it. The user is effectively providing input for a program on this remote computer. It sends a reply.

9. The remote modem turns the reply into a phone signal.

10. The user's modem turns it into data.

11. The telecommunications program interprets it and displays it as appropriate on the user's computer.

12. Eventually, one of the modems disconnects (hangs up) when told to by its computer's program.

TYPES OF MODEMS

Modems have evolved over the years, getting faster, cheaper, and sometimes smaller. They all still serve the same basic purpose: hooking up computers over long distances as if they were hooked up locally via their serial ports.

PC modems are divided into three types—internal, external, and acoustic.

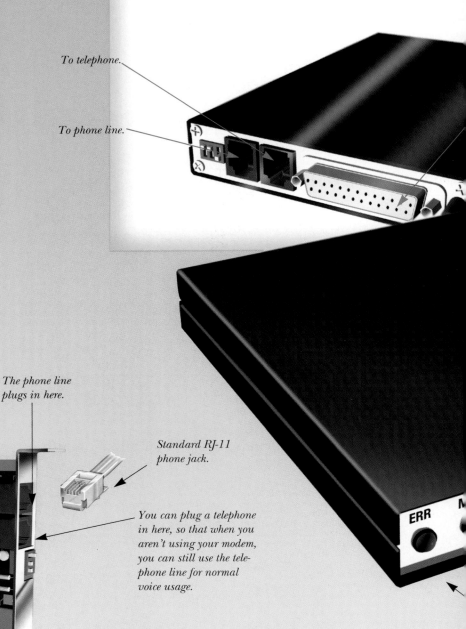

To telephone.

To phone line.

The speaker turns on to let you hear the modem connection being made.

The phone line plugs in here.

Standard RJ-11 phone jack.

You can plug a telephone in here, so that when you aren't using your modem, you can still use the telephone line for normal voice usage.

ERR

Internal modems go into a slot in your computer. These are cheaper than other modems, and don't tie up one of your serial ports (although because it is emulating a serial port device, your computer will give the internal modem a COM port number).

To computer's serial port.

External modems hook up to the serial port of the computer. These are popular not only because they can be hooked up to any type of computer with a serial port, but also because they have LEDs that display all kinds of status information—the modem speed, whether the modem is set up to answer the phone, and the state of the signals on various wires of the serial connection.

FACTS

One variation available in both external and internal modems is the *fax modem*. These work as standard modems, but also turn your computer into a type of fax (facsimile) machine, with the help of appropriate programs.

Instead of taking an image off of paper, as normal fax machines do, a computer with a fax modem sends pictures and text stored in computer files. So you can write a letter with your word processing program and print it somewhere via a modem, without having to print it out.

When you receive a fax, it doesn't go right to paper. Instead, it gets stored as a picture in a file. If you want to, you can print it out on your printer (which generally uses nicer paper then a fax machine does).

RX CD OH HS PWR

Modem status lights.

To computer.

Acoustic modems are obsolete, but still in use in some places. The telephone is dialed, and then the phone handset is stuck into the modem's cradle. Instead of turning electrical signals from the computer into electrical signals on the phone line, the electrical signal is turned into sound coming out of the speaker, which goes into the phone mouthpiece so the phone turns it into the phone line signal. Similarly, incoming data comes out of the earpiece and goes into a microphone in the modem.

MODULATION

The word *modem* is derived from two words. *Modulate* means to adapt and to vary the pitch of a sound. A modem adapts data from the cable to a telephone line by creating a tone of varying pitch. *Demodulate* means to do the opposite. A modem does both—modulating data going out and interpreting the modulated data that comes in.

Data is turned into sound waves. Bits are encoded as changes in three measurements of the waves.

Frequency is how long a whole wave takes.

Amplitude is how big the sound wave is.

Phase is the spacing between two similar waves.

By using combinations of these three elements, more than one bit can be sent simultaneously. The exact combination depends on the speed of the modem connection.

The receiving microphone takes the tones and, by measuring the frequency, amplitude, and phase, decodes the data being sent.

FACTS

The term *baud rate* is a bit confusing. Early modems could only send out one bit at a time, so the baud rate and the bits per second measurement were the same. People got used to using "baud" when referring to how fast the modem could send data. So when people mention 2,400 baud or 14,400 baud modems, what they are talking about is *bits per second*.

Remember that the modem is sending serial port data. As you learned in the serial port section, serial data has extra bits attached to each character—start bits, stop bits, and sometimes parity bits. Using the most common serial setting of 8 bits per character, no parity bit, 1 stop bit, each byte of data sent actually takes up 10 bits: the start bit, the 8 data bits, and the stop bit. So a modem communicating at 2,400 bits per second actually only sends 2400/10 or 240 data bytes per second.

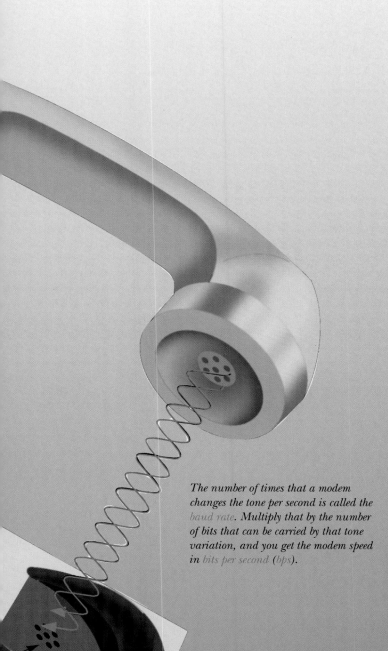

The number of times that a modem changes the tone per second is called the baud rate. Multiply that by the number of bits that can be carried by that tone variation, and you get the modem speed in bits per second (bps).

While acoustic modems are out of date, that's because they are the simplest modems, which makes them useful for illustration purposes. Non-acoustic modems work very similarly — they just skip turning the data into audible sound, and put it directly onto the phone line instead.

When you talk on the telephone, sometimes you will get some static, clicking, or other forms of what technical folks call line noise. If it's loud and long enough, it can make it hard to hear what the other person is saying.

Modems speak faster and listen more carefully then you do. Little bits of line noise can greatly confuse the demodulation of the data. This may not be a problem if you are just reading a message on a computer bulletin board, but if you are sending a file, this can be disastrous. If the file you are sending is a program, for example, as little as one garbled bit can make the program misbehave or not work at all. Even if you do find out that something is wrong with the file, you would probably have to send the whole thing over again, which could take a lot of time.

To avoid this problem, file transfer protocols were developed. These are systems of breaking files into smaller sections called packets, and making sure that each packet arrives with its data intact. Using the file transfer protocol requires that the communications programs on both ends know the protocol.

TRANSFER PROTOCOLS

Each protocol packages the data differently. Generally, header information identifies the packet...

...then there is the data...

Line noise.

...then the checksum, a number calculated from the binary values of all of the bits of data.

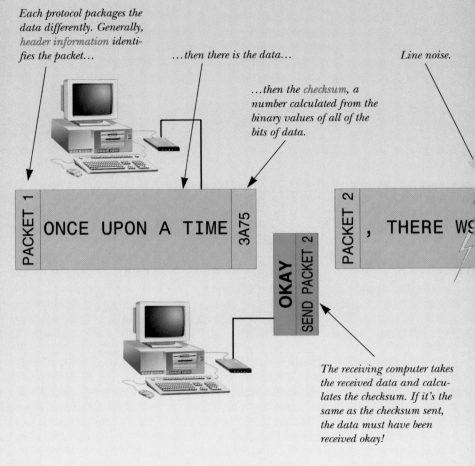

The receiving computer takes the received data and calculates the checksum. If it's the same as the checksum sent, the data must have been received okay!

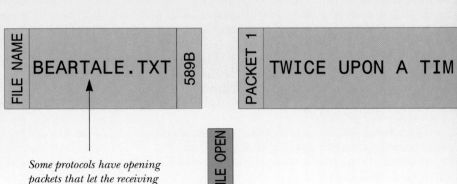

Some protocols have opening packets that let the receiving computer know the file name.

FACTS

Most protocols use a two-byte checksum that is computed in a way that makes sure that if any one of the bits goes wrong, the checksum will be different. Even if a whole bunch of bits are wrong, the odds of accidentally getting the same checksum are 1 in 65,536 (which is the number of different two-byte combinations that are possible).

The most popular protocols are those based on the old style protocol Xmodem. These include WXModem, YModem, and Zmodem, a full-blown new style protocol which can even continue a file transfer that was interrupted by one of the modems hanging up!

Other file transfer protocols are particularly popular for specific uses. Kermit is popular for transferring files with a UNIX system. The CompuServe Information Service has its own CompuServe B series of protocols. Most communications programs can understand a few of these protocols.

If a proper response isn't heard, the sending computer assumes that the packet wasn't understood and resends it.

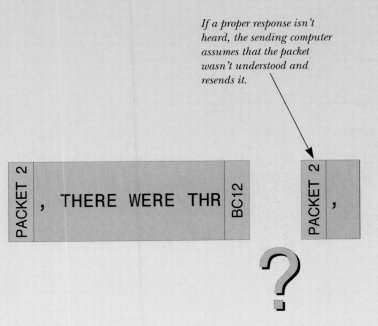

Older protocols are similar to two people talking, where one is talking a lot, and the other one is just saying "okay" to everything he understands, and "what?" to anything he doesn't.

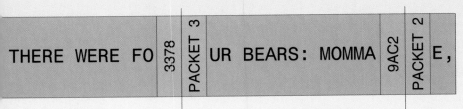

Older protocols wasted a lot of time waiting for the packet to travel over the phone system, for the receiving computer to check the checksum, and for the response to be sent. The newer protocols just keep sending data, rather than waiting.

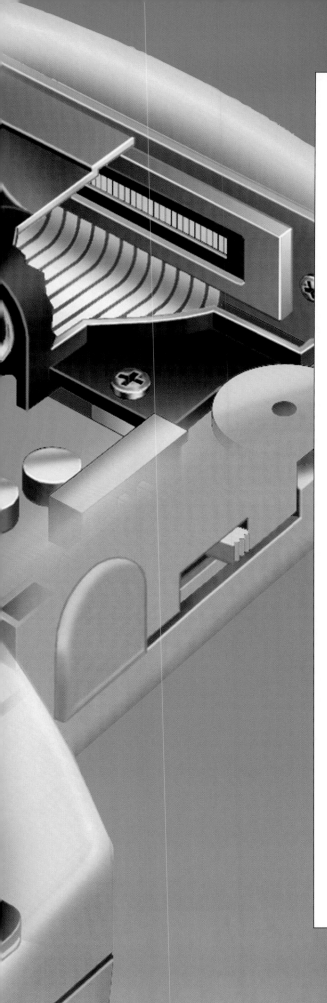

14

WHAT HAPPENS WHEN YOU USE YOUR SCANNER?

Hand Scanners and Flatbed Scanners

Optical Character Recognition

WHAT HAPPENS WHEN YOU USE YOUR SCANNER?

So far, we have covered a wide range of ways to change documents on a computer, and to get documents out of a computer and on paper. However, there are a lot of documents out there that aren't in computerized form that might be nice to get into the computer. Of course, you could retype the document on the computer, or redraw it entirely but that's a lot of work, and the point of having a computer is to make your life easier, not harder. Instead, you scan using a scanner.

A scanner scans over the page, pulling a picture off of the page and sending it to the computer, where it can be stored and manipulated.

The scanner goes over the page, interpreting it as a series of lines made up of individual dots of different colors or shades of gray.

The scanner program on the computer receives the image and allows you to store all or a portion of it for use with other programs that use pictures.

OCR programs allow you to separate out the text in the original document and store it in ASCII format, to be used with other text programs

HAND SCANNERS AND FLATBED SCANNERS

The most affordable scanners are hand scanners. These are simple, hand-held devices which are dragged across the page you wish to scan.

Because of this, the clarity of the image depends to a degree on the smoothness and steadiness of the dragging motion. Newer models make a straight, smooth drag easier, and perform better when the drag isn't smooth.

Flatbed scanners automate the process—making smoother scans—and can scan a full page at a time. They cost more but, for those with more than casual scanning needs, are generally worth the added cost.

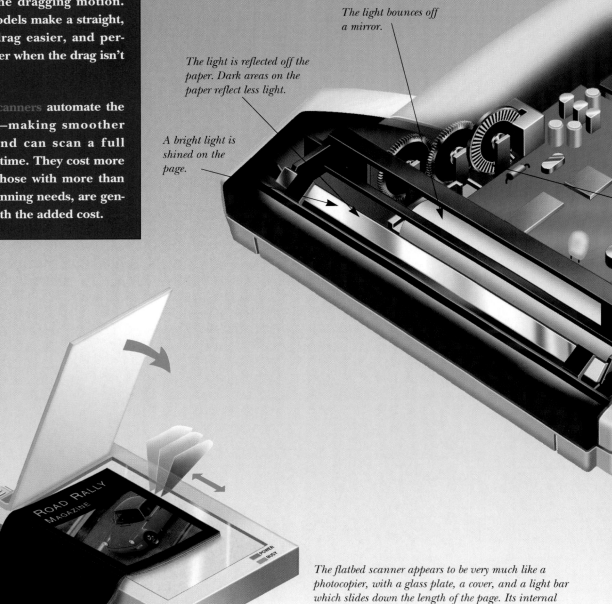

The light bounces off a mirror.

The light is reflected off the paper. Dark areas on the paper reflect less light.

A bright light is shined on the page.

ROAD RALLY MAGAZINE

POWER
BUSY

The flatbed scanner appears to be very much like a photocopier, with a glass plate, a cover, and a light bar which slides down the length of the page. Its internal workings, however, are very much like that of the hand scanner.

FACTS

Scanners are rated by two factors: the size of the grid that they break the image into, and how many different shades those dots can be.

The grid size is measured in dots per inch. Usually, a single number refers to both the horizontal and vertical measurements.

The number of shades on a non-color scanner is referred to as the gray scale. It will be a power of 2 (256, for example), since a fixed number of bits will be used.

Color resolution is referred to by the number of bits or the total number of colors those bits can represent (8-bit color is the same as 256 colors).

Just because your scanner uses a high resolution doesn't mean that you'll be able to take full advantage of it. For example, if you scan a 4-inch-by-4-inch photograph with a 256 gray scale setting, then you are generating 5 megabytes worth of data. While some compression can be done, this still may be too much data for your system to easily handle. High-powered graphic work calls for a system with a lot of RAM, and fills up a lot of disk space.

A lens focuses the light on the sensor array.

This bank of light sensors detects the level of reflected light.

The hand scanner is on a roller that is connected by gears to a slotted wheel. This wheel works just like the one inside an opti-mechanical mouse to track the speed and distance of the scanner's motion.

Red Separation

Green Separation

Blue Separation

Both flatbed and hand scanners are available that handle color. They separately measure the amount of red, green, and blue light reflected, and the program combines that into a single image.

OPTICAL CHARACTER RECOGNITION

When a scanner scans a page of text, it sees just a bunch of little dots. In order to turn this into ASCII characters that can be moved into word processing or another text handling program, it has to figure out which letters all those little dots stand for.

This is something you do all the time. You're doing it right now—as you read these words, your brain is thinking of these squiggles of inks as individual letters, and recognizing the words that they group into. It's so easy, you rarely think about the process. You probably only think of it when you are faced with a new, strange type style, where the letters are

Hard to recognize.

All typefaces are hard for a computer to understand. While people can generalize that a vertical line with a horizontal line near the top is a *T*, even recognizing the vertical and horizontal lines in a bunch of dots requires tricky programming, and allowing for all the little variations in letter shapes makes it tougher still.

Because it is so difficult, optical character recognition (OCR)—the ability to recognize letters and other characters from a picture—is still a growing science. New programs keep coming out that can read the letters more accurately than older programs.

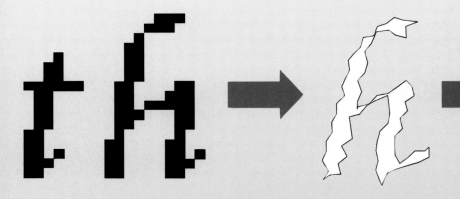

First, the program isolates all the dots belonging to each letter…

…then the program figures out the outline of that letter, to see it as a shape, rather than as a bunch of individual dots.

HEX 68

The computer then stores the ASCII value for that character, and goes on to the next letter in the scanned image.

The result is compared against a library of character shapes which the program has stored, to see which it is most like.

FACTS

Even if you just need to store a document on your hard disk, and you will never need to edit it or use the text from it in any way, it still makes sense to run it through an OCR program. The text file will be much smaller than the file of the picture of the page—each letter in the text file is just 8 bits, while the picture of that letter probably takes up hundreds.

The ability of the OCR software to recognize the character is improved by a higher-resolution scan.

Every character recognized is a guess: *"It looks a lot like an h, but not much like anything else."* A good OCR program will be pretty sure of most of its guesses, but when it isn't, it might be able to point you to the characters that it is unsure about.

OCR software has gotten good enough at recognizing printed text that it is quite reasonable to scan a document in. However, handwriting recognition is another problem entirely, since handwriting is more variable and tends to be sloppy. To get a handwritten document into a computer accurately, it's still best to retype it. Fancy typefaces, like the ones many magazines use, also are difficult. Advanced OCR software can learn new typefaces for its library.

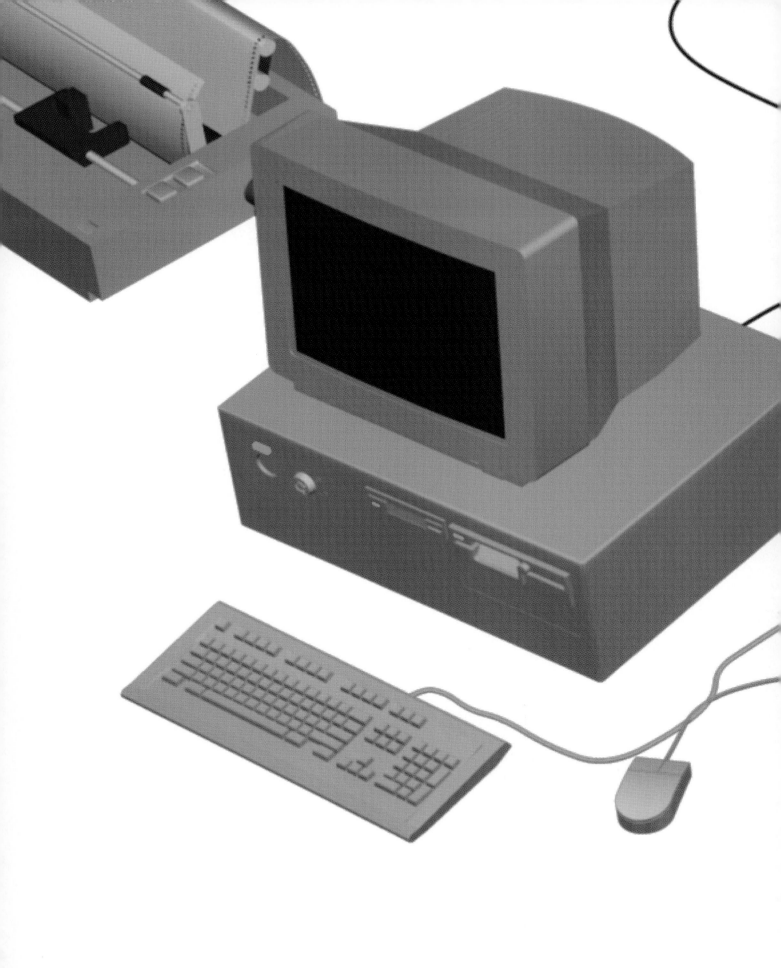

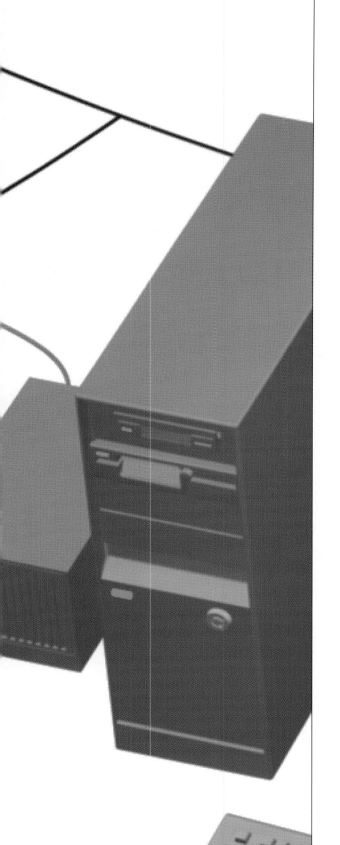

CHAPTER

15

WHAT HAPPENS WHEN YOU CONNECT TO A LOCAL AREA NETWORK?

The Physical Network

The Logical Network

WHAT HAPPENS WHEN YOU CONNECT TO A LOCAL AREA NETWORK?

It used to be that a business would have one central computer, and everyone would use separate terminals that worked on that computer. All files were stored on that system, and everyone who was connected to the computer shared the printer. But when stand-alone PCs began arriving, what was to be done about the files everyone needed to share? And if there weren't printers for everyone, how would everyone print? The quick answer was for people to pass around shared files on floppy disks, and if you needed to print something, go to a PC which had a printer, wait until someone else wasn't using it, and then print your document. This made for a lot of running around, and a lot of waiting.

Local area networks (LANs) solve the problem of how to share files and computer resources. A LAN is a system of cables and cards that links a group of computers together. The computers can exchange information over these cables, so that files stored on one system are available to all. Programs can be written to interact directly with programs running on other computers, at much higher speeds than if they were linked together by a modem.

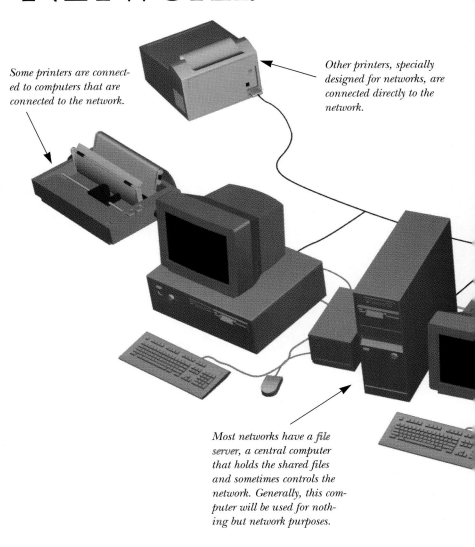

Some printers are connected to computers that are connected to the network.

Other printers, specially designed for networks, are connected directly to the network.

Most networks have a file server, a central computer that holds the shared files and sometimes controls the network. Generally, this computer will be used for nothing but network purposes.

The cables are run through walls and in ceilings to reach many rooms. Some newer buildings have network sockets built into the walls, just like electrical sockets.

Other networks have no central server. Instead, the files are spread among the various computer's hard disks.

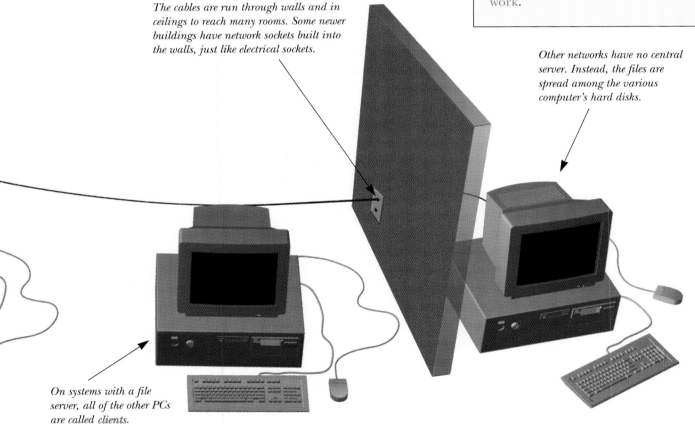

On systems with a file server, all of the other PCs are called clients.

While a standard is designed to make sure different pieces can work together, there are a large number of different standards for networking—and pieces from different standards won't work together. All of the pieces of your network must share the same standard for the physical cabling, and share the same standard for how they communicate over those cables.

THE PHYSICAL NETWORK

All PCs hooked to a network need a network interface card, which provides the physical connection to the network and handles much of the work of conversing over the network.

Other networks are wired together in a star configuration. All of the client computers connect directly to the file server or to a special device called a repeater. This hub gets a message from one of the outlying computers, sees what computer or printer it is directed to, and puts it out on the right cable.

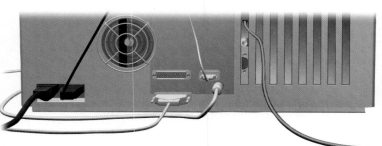

FACTS

A star network is easy to maintain—if one computer is having trouble communicating, it is pretty clear that the problem must be in that computer, or its cable to the hub. However, the entire network depends on that hub. If that breaks down in some way, the network is useless. Plus, every device needs cables running all the way to the hub.

When you chain PCs together with EtherNet cables, you only need enough cable to reach the nearest PC in the network. If any of the computers breaks down, the network goes on working; you just can't get files from the broken computer. On the other hand, when you start having communications problems, it can be difficult to track down which piece in the chain is causing the problem.

Manufacturers have come out with wireless network systems, which use small radio transceivers to send messages from computer to computer. Others have even come up with networks that use the electrical wiring running through your building. These are just a few of the many alternative wiring systems available.

Another popular cabling system is twisted pair cable, which gets its name because the cable has wires twisted together in pairs.

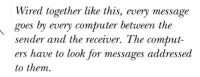

Wired together like this, every message goes by every computer between the sender and the receiver. The computers have to look for messages addressed to them.

The most common physical cabling system is thin EtherNet. The cable used is coaxial cable, similar to that used for cable television.

The T-shaped connector that the EtherNet cable hooks into lets all the PCs in a network be hooked together in a chain.

THE LOGICAL NETWORK

The software to hook your computer up to a LAN is quite complex. It has to be able to translate your program's requests for disk access into messages on the network, and to feed your computer the data that pours in from the network. On the system that receives the request for disk access, the network messages must get translated into disk commands that the operating system understands.

To the programs that you run, all the hard disks accessible on the network look like they are hard disks on your computer.

Each computer has a driver program that lets it talk to the network.

NETWORK DRIVER

The network interface card passes on the requests to read and write files to the network.

ENTER FILE TO LOAD:
F:/letters/iloveu.wp

The network interface card handles the basic levels of communication— finding the messages addressed to your computer, checking to make sure that the messages came through clear-ly, and passing all information from the line to the driver program.

FACTS

While a lot of effort has gone into making networks easier to set up and manage, they are still complex. When setting up a significant new network, most businesses hire a network consultant, who will help you pick the right network for your needs and get it running as efficiently as possible.

Another part of the network driver handles requests from other computers to work with the data on your disk drive.

The information is managed on the line in a manner very similar to the file transfer protocols discussed in Chapter 13; it is broken down into packets, with header information and a checksum. Plus, since there are generally more than two devices being connected, there are addresses—special numbers to indicate where the message is coming from and going to.

A response is sent to acknowledge that the message was received.

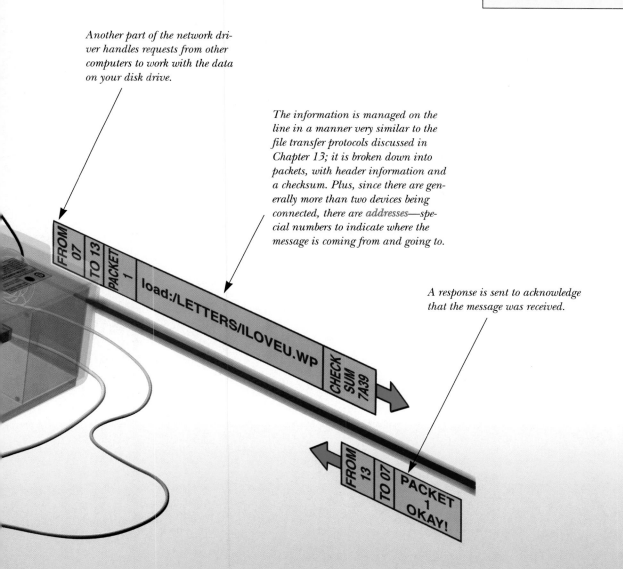

DOS USER COMMAND PROCESSOR

DOS SYSTEM

HARD

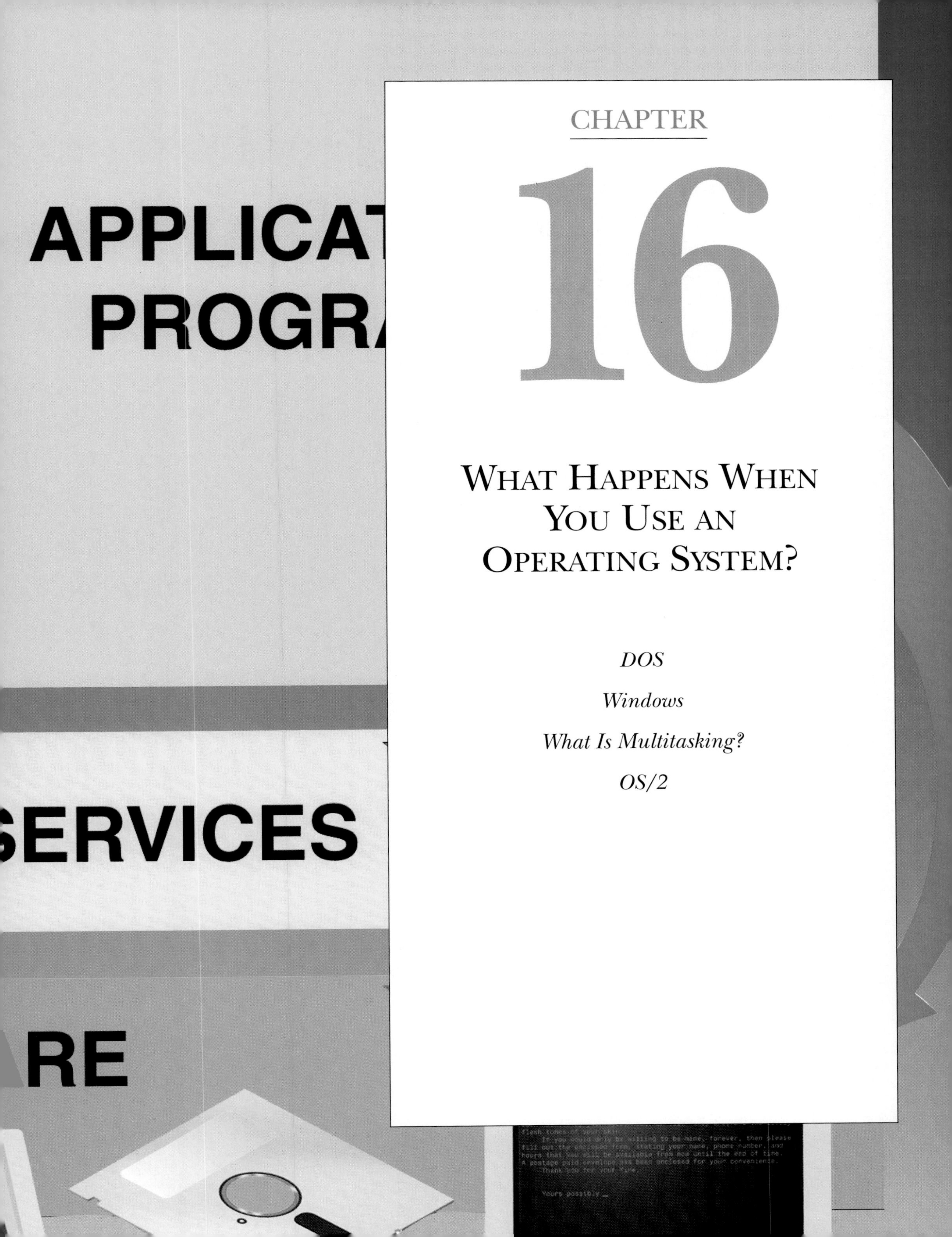

APPLICAT
PROGRA

SERVICES

RE

16

WHAT HAPPENS WHEN YOU USE AN OPERATING SYSTEM?

DOS

Windows

What Is Multitasking?

OS/2

WHAT HAPPENS WHEN YOU USE AN OPERATING SYSTEM?

Many users think of the operating system (OS) simply as the program that is running when nothing else is. That idea seems correct because that's when the operating system is most visible, but the operating system is running even when another program is running. It's providing a full set of tools that the program can use for dealing with all the various parts of the computer and its peripherals.

The user commands portion of the operating system allows the user to control the system in various ways—copying files, setting the system clock, etc. It uses the services just like any other program does.

DOS USER COMMAND PROCESSOR

The operating system provides a series of special functions or services for dealing with input and output, particularly with the disk drives. This lets a program issue a simple command for something like creating a new file, and the operating system takes care of all the dirty work.

DOS

Because the application lets the operating system handle certain functions, changing how the operating system handles something will change it for all programs. Disk compression programs are a clear example of this.

Some programs cheat, accessing hardware directly instead of going through the operating system. This often lets them work faster, but can cause compatibility problems.

APPLICATION PROGRAM

TEM SERVICES

RDWARE

FACTS

Because the operating system is just a big program, different operating systems can be designed to run on the same type of computer. Only one operating system at a time is actually controlling the system. Multiple operating systems can be stored on a single hard drive.

Any program that the user wants to run has to be designed to run on a specific operating system, so that it knows what operating system commands to expect, and it will have functions that the operating system expects to find.

Many operating systems have been created for IBM-compatible personal computers. Most of them go unnoticed by the vast majority of users. People aren't going to use operating systems that don't run the programs that they need to use. Companies won't write programs for operating systems that the user isn't going to have. As such, it is hard to make a new operating system successful.

DOS

DOS (rhymes with *gloss*; it stands for *Disk Operating System*) is how most people refer to the operating system which Microsoft sells as MS-DOS (*Microsoft DOS*) and IBM sells as PC DOS (*Personal Computer DOS*). Both of these are the same core operating system, developed by Microsoft at IBM's behest.

DOS's natural user interface is text-only.

DOS sets certain standards, like the standard file name format, so that both the program and the user know what to expect.

The command line offers no suggestions for what the user might do. This is intimidating to new users, but a comfort to many experienced users who feel that fancy graphic interfaces slow things down.

```
C:\PICTURES>dir

 Volume in drive
 Directory of  C

.                 <DIP
..                <DIP
HEART      PIC
FLOWERS    PIC
FLOWERS2   PIC
WINE       PIC    2
PAINTER    EXE    6
README     TXT
RUNME      BAT
CHEESE     PIC
        9 File(s)

C:\PICTURES>
C:\PICTURES>pain
```

The top 6 segments of the megabyte are reserved for special purposes.

The CPUs that DOS runs on deal with memory in 64K chunks called segments.

DOS expects programs and data in the first 10 segments.

Extended memory is memory past the first megabyte that newer CPUs can deal with directly, even if the operating system cannot understand it.

STANDARD MEMORY (640K)	RESERVED MEMORY (384K)	EXTENDED MEMORY

EXPANDED MEMORY

DOS was designed for a CPU that could handle only one megabyte of memory. Many things can be done with more memory, but certain things still have to be in that first megabyte. It's easy to write operating systems that go beyond the one megabyte limit, but all existing software is designed around the standards set by that limit, and actually require it to be in place.

Expanded memory is a system of disguising selected quarter segments of extra memory as standard memory. The special expanded memory board or software driver can change which quarter segments are disguised as standard memory, thus allowing commands designed to work with standard memory awkward access to large amounts of extra memory.

```
o label
ES

7-03-93    11:28a
7-03-93    11:28a
1-05-93     5:08p
9-03-93     8:26a
8-17-93     4:29p
9-13-93     9:59a
1-08-93     3:31p
1-05-93     5:07p
9-13-93    12:37p
9-13-93     9:53a
56 bytes free
```

DOS is designed to run only one standard program at a time. Special programs can run along with a standard program, taking control whenever DOS uses an operating system function (when it writes information to the disk, for example, or awaits input from the keyboard) or when the operating system interrupts the program.

FACTS

Microsoft's original design for MS-DOS was based heavily on an earlier operating system, CP/M. CP/M was designed by Digital Research to operate microprocessor chips that could handle only 64K of memory. In the early days of the IBM PC, Digital Research did its own version of CP/M for this new machine, called CP/M-86, but it never became as popular as DOS.

Digital Research returned the compliment by creating its own operating system modeled after DOS. DR-DOS (pronounced either *dee-are-dos* or *doctor dos*) runs on the same machines as MS-DOS and provides the same services, so it can run programs designed around the other operating system. Then, networking giant Novell (pronounced *know-vel*) bought the rights to the operating system and released it as Novell DOS, with even further improvements. It competes with MS-DOS by being more affordable and adding more features, particularly network-related features.

The program in charge of the user interface is COMMAND.COM. Two programs stored in hidden files provide the operating system functions. In the IBM-produced versions, these are IBMBIO.COM and IBM-DOS.COM. In Microsoft versions, these are called IO.SYS and MSDOS.SYS. Operating systems come with many support files that allow additional capabilities.

WINDOWS

indows, the Microsoft package that allows you to run programs with a consistent graphical interface and with certain advanced capabilities, is *not* an operating system. The current versions are actually an operating environment, a set of programs that builds on an operating system, providing further tools, functions, and standards that programs designed for that environment can use.

Windows 3.1, the most popular version of the environment, runs with the standard DOS operating system. It can run specially designed Windows programs, which take advantage of its special features. It also can add features to most programs designed to run directly with DOS.

Once running, Windows can load other programs in the same way that some programs can load overlays.

Windows looks like a single program to DOS, keeping within its "one program at a time" rule.

Windows provides a lot of additional tools for the programs to count on. The most obvious of these are the ones that control how the program interacts with the user. By using these tools, the program can be sure that it looks and works similar to all other Windows programs, making it easier to use.

Windows depends on the operating system's tools.

WINDOWS APPLICATION PROGRAM

SERVICES FOR WINDOWS

DOS USER COMMAND PROCESSOR

DO

Newer CPUs can simulate a virtual machine, which appears to the programs in it like they are running on their own computer, without any other programs. A version of DOS runs in that virtual machine, and standard DOS programs run in it. By intercepting the program's attempts to access DOS functions, Windows takes some control over the program and its display.

Windows can load multiple programs at once.

Windows expects the program to supply certain standard tools of its own that the environment can access. This lets it do things like read data from one program and put it into another.

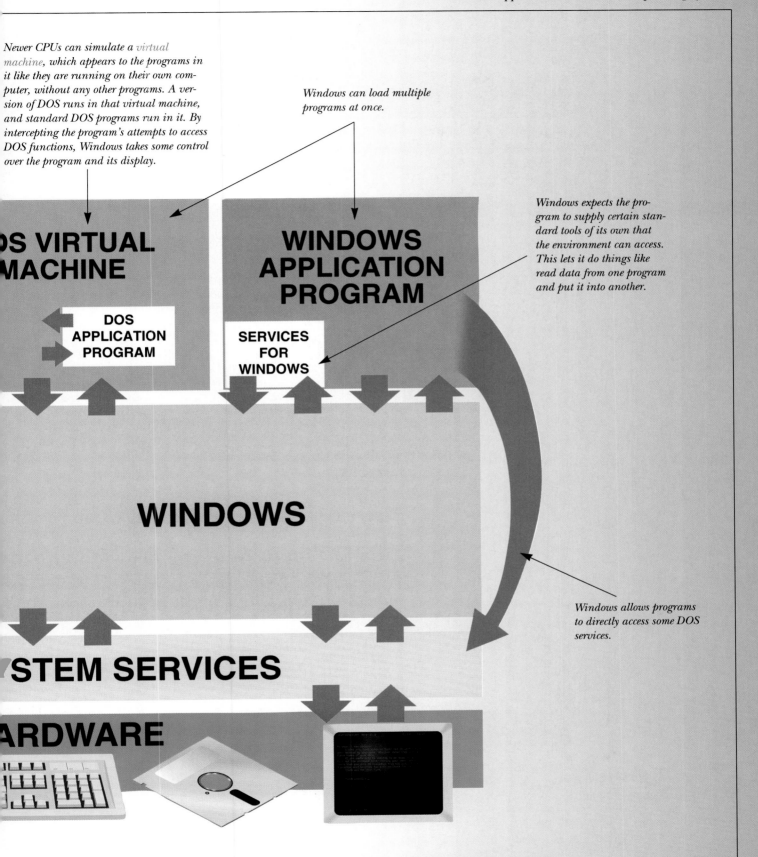

OS VIRTUAL MACHINE

WINDOWS APPLICATION PROGRAM

DOS APPLICATION PROGRAM

SERVICES FOR WINDOWS

WINDOWS

STEM SERVICES

ARDWARE

Windows allows programs to directly access some DOS services.

Standard DOS programs don't have the calls for the special user interface routines, so the user inputs data and controls them just like without Windows. Windows does add some capabilities in controlling these programs, such as the ability to resize the screen, and the ability to copy information from the DOS program's display.

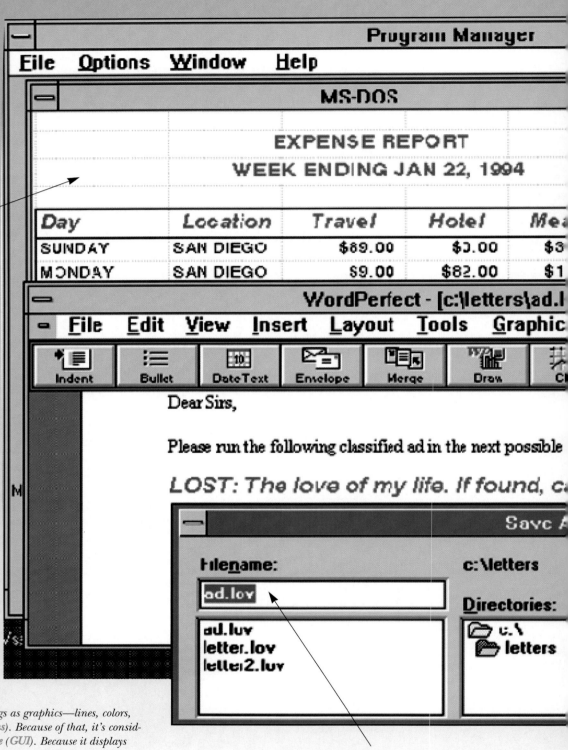

Windows displays many things as graphics—lines, colors, and little pictures (called *icons*). Because of that, it's considered a *graphical user interface (GUI)*. Because it displays information in rectangular areas called *windows*, and it displays icons and uses the mouse to move a *pointer* around the screen, the user interface also is referred to as a *windows/icon/mouse/pointer (WIMP)* interface.

Because Windows operates under DOS, most DOS limitations are still in effect. For example, file names are still limited to eight characters with a three character extension.

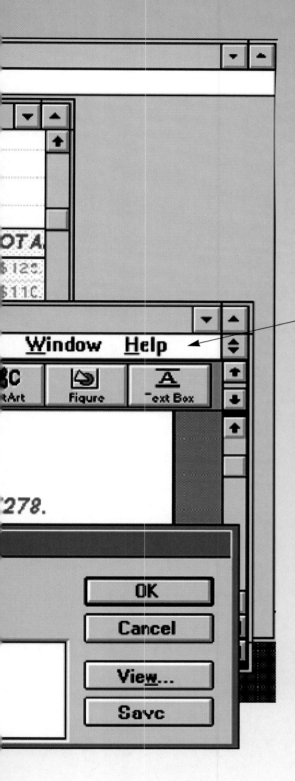

The word processing program tells the operating environment that it needs a menu with these elements. The operating environment displays the menu, recognizes when the user selects an item from the menu, and passes that information on to the word processing program. You can use the mouse to operate the menu, or you can hold down the Alt key and press the underlined letter to get the same effect.

FACTS

Microsoft is working to evolve Windows from an operating environment to a full-fledged operating system.

Windows requires a lot of computing power. To run it well, you need a powerful CPU, megabytes of RAM, and lots of hard disk space. Many machines simply cannot run Windows.

With the operating environment supplying the user interface, it would seem that programs designed to run in that environment would be smaller than their DOS-only counterparts. Actually, the opposite is true, because Windows expects the programs to have a lot of special features built in that only it needs.

If the concept of a graphical environment sounds enticing to you, but your machine is not powerful enough for Windows, there are other options. GeoWorks is a popular environment because, while it does not provide the full features of Windows, it is a much smaller, tighter, faster program, and can run on many machines that cannot handle Windows. Unfortunately, there are not very many programs designed to run in the GeoWorks environment.

WHAT IS MULTITASKING?

T he faster technology gets, the more quickly we become impatient with it. Maybe you have found yourself tapping your fingers, waiting for the fax machine to finish a page—a message that a few years ago would have taken days to send across the country. Despite the fact that computers are faster than ever, we can quickly grow irritated when waiting for them, particularly when printing something or doing something that requires a lot of disk accessing.

But the computer is waiting, too! The CPU goes a lot faster than the peripherals, and spends a lot of time waiting for them.

The spreadsheet is in the middle of a huge calculation. That takes pure CPU power; it's not waiting for any peripheral.

DATABASE PROGRAM

SPREADSHEET PROGRAM

```
                          .
                          .
                          .
    REQUEST FILE FROM DISK    CALCULATE
                          .   CALCULATE
    WAIT FOR FILE             CALCULATE
                          .   CALCULATE
                          .   CALCULATE
                          .   CALCULATE
                          .   CALCULATE
                          .   CALCULATE
                          .
                              .
                              .
                              .
```

The database program is waiting for some information that it requested from the hard disk. When the CPU sees that it is waiting for information that hasn't arrived, it moves on to the next program.

The CPU will keep going through the programs, doing a little bit of work, many times per second.

Some operating systems and environments support multitasking, *the ability to run more than one program at a time. The CPU can actually only do one thing at a time, but by spending a small fraction of a second on each program before going on to the next, it seems like it is doing several things simultaneously. Spending small amounts of time with each program is called* time slicing.

DATABASE PROGRAM

```
                          .
                          .
                          .
    REQUEST FILE FROM DISK
    WAIT FOR FILE
                          .
                          .
                          .
                          .
```

With an operating system that only runs one program at a time, the CPU has nothing to do but wait while the peripheral is doing something.

After a set amount of time running one program, the CPU knows it's time to move on to the next program.

Word processing programs spend most of their time waiting for the slowest component of any computer system— the user. While it may seem to you that you are typing fast, to the computer it seems like an eternity between keystrokes, time that it can use to run other programs.

WORD PROCESSING PROGRAM

EDITING SUBPROGRAM

WAIT FOR KEYSTROKE

INSERT LETTER

UPDATE DISPLAY

PRINTING SUBPROGRAM

PRINTALINE:
GET NEXT LINE TO PRINT

WAIT FOR PRINTER
TO BE READY

SEND LINE TO PRINTER

IF MORE LINES,
GO TO PRINTALINE

Some multitasking systems can actually be sharing time between different routines in the same program. This is called multithreading.

One program is always selected as being in the foreground. This means this is the program that gets any information the user types, even if other programs are waiting for keyboard input.

FACTS

Some systems require that the program stop itself from time to time to check if its slice of time is up. This is called cooperative multitasking, since the program has to cooperate with the system in letting the multitasking take place. A badly written program won't check to see if its time is up, and will tie up the whole system, not letting any other program get work done. Windows is an example of cooperative multitasking.

Other systems have the ability to stop processing a given program automatically after a set amount of time, whether the program cooperates or not. This is called preemptive multitasking, as the system can preempt what the individual program is trying to do. OS/2, discussed in the next section, is an example of this.

Even in a single-tasking system, talented programmers can pull tricks that make it seem like a program is multithreading. A lot of DOS word processing programs and spreadsheets, for example, can print one file while you edit another (a process called background printing). The difference is that the program itself, rather than the operating system or environment, must manage switching between the two different parts of the program.

OS/2

Each new generation of CPU makes possible more powerful programs, but the operating systems that are designed around the older CPUs won't let programs take full advantage of the new CPU.

OS/2 is an IBM operating system designed to take advantage of more modern CPUs than what DOS was designed for. It's capable of running programs that use the 32-bit functions of the processor, manipulating values four bytes at a time. (They're still all made up of single-bit operations, of course.)

OS/2 has preemptive multitasking and multithreading. IBM worked hard at making sure that, while it had power, it also could run programs designed for DOS, so that it didn't depend on people creating special OS/2 applications for it to be usable.

Because it isn't based around DOS, OS/2 doesn't have DOS limitations. File names can be up to 254 characters long.

Like Windows, OS/2 can create virtual DOS machines for running DOS applications.

Most users use OS/2's graphical user interface, called Presentation Manager, which is needed to run many programs. Other programs, however, can be run in OS/2's text mode, a character-based interface more like DOS than like Windows.

FACTS

It always takes a while for the companies making operating systems and other software to take full advantage of a new CPU, because you really can't start programming around features of a chip until the chip is available. Large programs take a long time to develop. The current OS/2 is really designed to take maximum advantage of the 80386, and while it runs even faster on the newer CPUs (the 486 and the Pentium), it doesn't take full advantage of all their new features.

Presentation Manager requires more memory than the DOS/Windows combination, as well as needing a reasonably powerful CPU. Most users considering switching to OS/2 will have to add at least more memory, and might possibly need a whole new computer.

Microsoft is countering OS/2 with Windows NT, which is related to its Windows operating environment, but is a full and powerful operating system.

OS/2 can even run a version of Windows, allowing it to run most Windows programs.

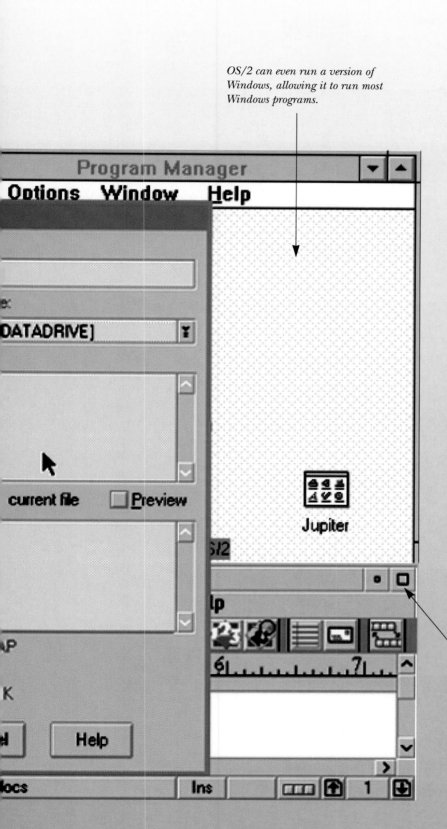

OS/2 programs use menus and windowing controls very similar to Windows.

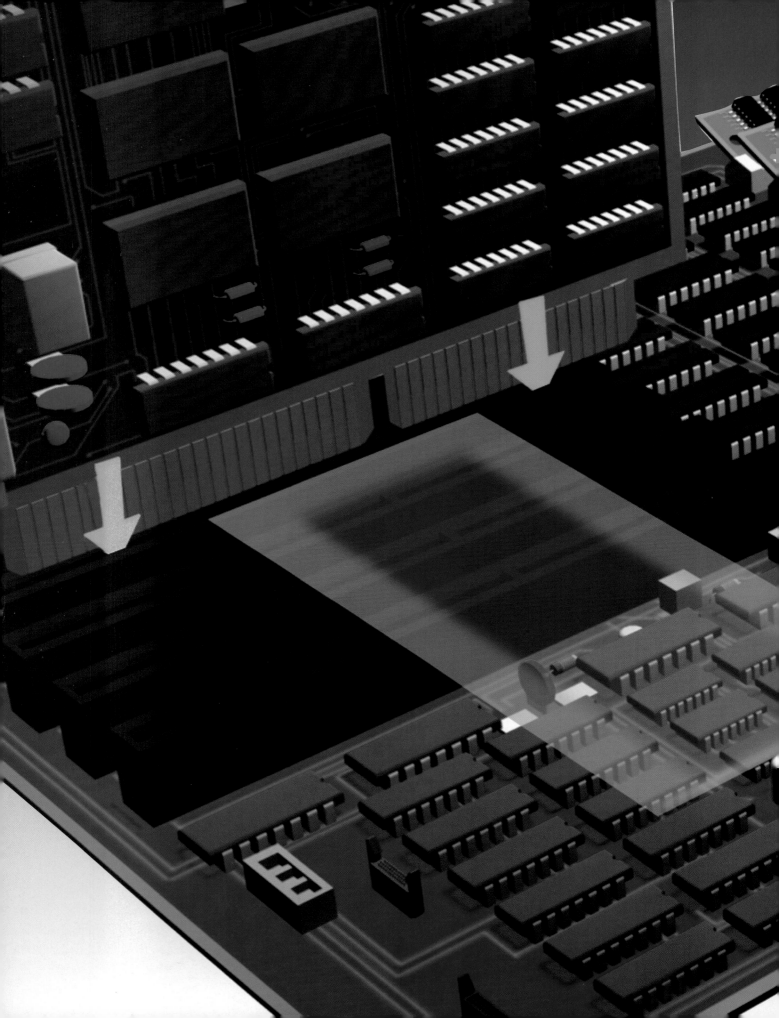

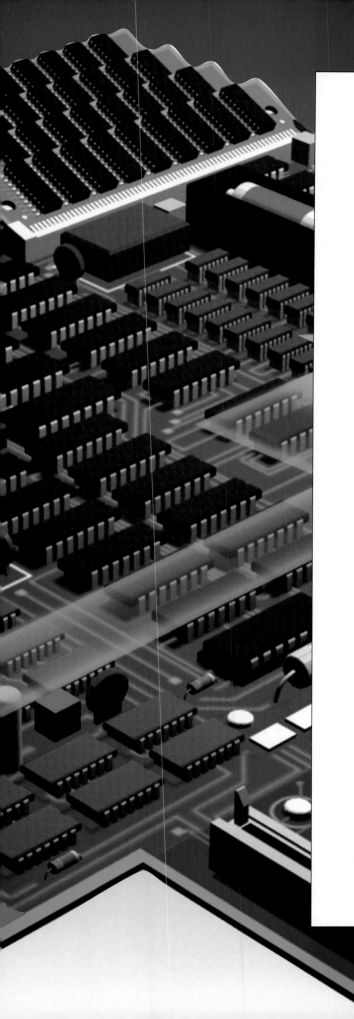

GLOSSARY

101–key enhanced keyboard A current standard in keyboard design for keyboards supporting a large number of different keys. See "The Keyboard," p. 86.

access time Average time it takes for a given hard disk to move the read/write head into position to read a requested sector. See "Using Hard Drives," p. 122.

acknowledge line A line on a parallel connection which is used to indicate when the device is ready for more data. See "Parallel Ports," p. 156.

acoustic modem A modem which connects not to the phone line, but to the phone handset. See "Types of Modems," p. 178.

address A value that indicates a location in memory. See "Random-Access Memory," p. 48. Also, a value that indicates a specific device on a network. See "The Logical Network," p. 198.

adventure game A computer game which involves controlling a character through a series of challenges and puzzles. See "Games," p. 34.

amplitude The size of a wave. See "Modulation," p. 180.

analog Representing a value as an infinitely variable signal. See "Scanning Frequency," p. 150.

AND A logical operator that puts out the value of true (or 1) only if both values going in are true (or 1). See "Binary Logic," p. 14.

arcade game An action-oriented computer game. See "Games," p. 34.

archive utility A program which stores a group of files as a single, smaller file. See "File Compression," p. 110.

ASCII Abbreviation for American Standard Code for Information Interchange, a method of encoding text as binary values. See "All Information Is Numeric," p. 10.

assembler A program that takes a program written in assembly language and turns it into machine language. See "What Is a Computer Program?" p. 16.

auto feed pin A line on a parallel I/O connection, used by the computer to tell the printer whether to automatically advance the paper with each carriage return. See "Parallel Ports," p. 156.

AUTOEXEC.BAT A batch file program that is run by DOS at startup. See "The Operating System Adapts to You," p. 72.

background printing A feature which allows a file to be printed while the computer can still work on other processes. See "What Is Multitasking?," p. 210.

backup A stored duplicate copy of disk information. See "Tape Drives," p. 124.

base 2 See *binary*.

base 16 See *hexadecimal*.

batch files Programs written as a series of commands interpreted by the operating system. See "The Operating System Adapts to You," p. 72.

baud A measurement of how many times per second a modem can send information, sometimes also used to mean *bits per second*. See "Modulation," p. 180.

BBS See *Bulletin Board System*.

binary A way of encoding numbers as a series of bits. See "What Are Binary Numbers," p. 12.

binary logic A system of logic built around comparisons between two bits. See "Binary Logic," p. 14.

BIOS Abbreviation for Basic Input/Output System, the program that controls the basic functions of communications between the processor and the I/O devices. See "The Basic Input/Output System," p. 68.

bit The smallest unit of information, which represents one of two values (usually 0 and 1). Also, the memory or disk space used to hold that information. See "What Are Binary Numbers," p. 12.

boot block The first sector of a disk, used to store the operating system loading programs. See "Sections of the Disk," p. 100.

bps Abbreviation for bits per second, a measurement of communication speed. See "Modulation," p. 180.

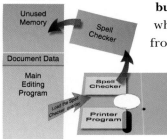

MEMORY

buffer A storage area of memory which holds information going from one place to another, until the receiving device is ready to accept it. See "Daisywheel Printers," p. 164.

Bulletin board system A computer set up to distribute messages over a modem. Abbreviated BBS. See "Telecommunications," p. 32.

burning ROMs Using a special device to store information in ROM chips. See "Read-Only Memory," p. 50.

busy line A communications line on a parallel connection used to tell the computer that the device is busy with the information it already received. See "Parallel Ports," p. 156.

byte Eight bits of information. A single byte can have 256 different values. See "What Are Binary Numbers," p. 12.

CAD See *Computer-aided design.*

carriage A metal rod in a printer the print head slides. See "Daisywheel Printers," p. 164

cathode A device that shoots out electrons. See "How Monitors Work," p. 144.

cathode ray tube The picture tube of a monitor. Abbreviated CRT. See "How Monitors Work," p. 144.

CD-ROM Abbreviation for Compact Disk Read-Only Memory. Optically readable disks used to distribute large amounts of information. See "CD-ROM," p. 126.

cell A single space on a spreadsheet grid. See "Doing Math," p. 28.

Central processing unit The main command-interpreting chip in a computer. Abbreviated CPU. See "The Central Processing Unit," p. 46.

Centronics-type connector A standard connector with 36 contacts, named after the printer manufacturer that developed it. See "Parallel Ports," p. 156.

CGA Abbreviation for Color Graphics Adapter, a low-quality standard for video adapters. See "What Happens When You Use Your Monitor?" p. 142.

checksum A value calculated on a set of data, and used to check the data's integrity. See "Transfer Protocols," p. 182.

chip A small flat square with silicon-based transistors used for logic or data storage; also, the casing on metal pins which contain the chip. See "Transistor Switches," p. 42.

CISC Abbreviation for Complex Instruction Set Computing, a philosophy of processor design that focuses on creating processors that handle a wide range of powerful instruction. See "The Central Processing Unit," p. 46.

clients Computers on a local area network which receive files from the file server. See "What Happens When You Connect to a Local Area Network?" p. 194.

clip art Existing art for use with computer art and desktop publication programs. See "Doing Math," p. 28.

cluster A group of disk sectors allocatable as a unit. See "Sections of the Disk," p. 100.

coaxial cable A type of cable used in cable TV connections and some local area networks. See "The Physical Network," p. 196.

cold boot Starting a computer by turning it on. See "Finding the Operating System," p. 70.

command An instruction given to the computer by the user or by a program. See "What Is a Computer?" p. 8.

COMMAND.COM The program that handles the DOS user interface. See "DOS," p. 204.

compiler A program that takes a program written in a programming language and translates it into machine language, so that the computer can understand it. See "What Is a Computer Program," p. 16.

CompuServe B A file transfer protocol. See "Transfer Protocols," p. 182.

computer A device which processes information.

computer-aided design The designing of physical objects using computer programs. Abbreviated CAD. See "Painting and Drawing," p. 30.

conductor A material that carries electricity well. See "Transistor Switches," p. 42.

CONFIG.SYS A file used in DOS to inform the system of the presence of special devices and to set up communications with those devices. See "The Operating System Adapts to You," p. 72.

cooperative multitasking A system of multitasking which requires that programs be designed to voluntarily return control to the operating system or environment at regular intervals. See "What Is Multitasking?," p. 210.

corona wire A wire which dissipates static charge from a laser printer's drum, clearing it for printing the next page. See "Laser Printers," p. 170.

CP/M An operating system used in older computers. See "DOS," p. 204.

CP/M—86 An early operating system for computers based around the 8086 CPU. See "DOS," p. 204.

CPU See *Central processing unit.*

cracker Someone who accesses computer systems without permission. See "What Happens When You Use Your Modem?" p. 176.

cradle The part of an acoustical modem in which the handset rests. See "Types of Modems," p. 178.

criteria A set of requirements for selecting an item from a group, as in selecting records from a database program. See "Keeping Records," p. 26.

CRT See *cathode ray tube.*

CTS Abbreviation for Clear To Send, the line in a serial I/O connection that the device uses to let the computer know that it is ready to receive data. See "Serial Ports," p. 158.

current directory The directory that your commands currently affect. See "How Directories Are Organized," p. 98.

cylinder A circular portion of all of the sides in a disk. See "What Happens When You Format a Disk?" p. 134.

daisywheel A disk with spokes coming out, with characters at the end of each spoke. This is part of a daisywheel printer. See "Daisywheel Printers," p. 164.

daisywheel printer An impact printer which uses a daisywheel to print a fixed set of characters. See "Daisywheel Printers," p. 164.

data Pieces of information. See "What Is a Computer?" p. 8.

data file A file which stores information for a program to process. See "Types of Files," p. 96.

database A set of records stored as a group. See "Keeping Records," p. 26.

database program A program designed to maintain a set of records and generate reports based on that information. See "Keeping Records," p. 26.

datum A single piece of information. See "What Is a Computer?" p. 8.

DB-9 A standard connector design with nine leads. See "Serial Ports," p. 158.

DB-25 A standard connector design with 25 leads. See "Parallel Ports," p. 156.

DCD Data Carrier Detect, the line on a serial connection used to indicate that a connection has been completed. See "Serial Ports," p. 158.

defragmenter A program which rearranges the files so that they are in contiguous clusters. See "Fragmented Files," p. 108.

delete To remove, as in *deleting* a file. See "Deleting a File," p. 106.

demodulate To decode information from modulated sound. See "Modulation," p. 180.

desktop computer A computer designed to sit on your desk. See "Basic Computer Anatomy," p. 38.

desktop publishing program A program that lets you design the layouts of printed pages. See "Desktop Publishing," p. 24.

digital Representing a value of something as one of a limited set of possible signals. See "Scanning Frequency," p. 150.

digitizing tablet An input device on which the user draws lines using a stylus. The lines then appear on-screen in computer art programs. See "Input Devices," p. 84.

directory A grouping of files on the disk. See "What Happens When Files Are Created?" p. 94.

directory tree The organizational structure of directories on a disk. See "How Directories Are Organized," p. 98.

disk A unit with one or more platters (or *discs*) which are used to store information. See "What Happens When You Use Your Disk Drives?" p. 116.

disk compression utility A program which reduces the amount of space that files take up on a hard drive. See "File Compression," p. 110.

disk drive A device used to read and store information on circular media. See "What Happens When You Use Your Disk Drives?" p. 116.

diskless PC A personal computer with no disk drives, designed to attach to a local area network and to use only files stored on other computers on that network. See "What Happens When You Connect to a Local Area Network?" p. 194.

DOS Disk Operating System, a term commonly used to refer to the operating system products MS-DOS and PC DOS. See "DOS," p. 204.

dot-matrix printer An impact printer which creates images as gridworks of dots. See "Dot-Matrix Printers," p. 166.

dot pitch The spacing between the pixels on a color monitor. See "Pixels and Resolution," p. 146.

double density Describes floppy disks physically capable of storing more information than regular-density disks but not as much as high-density disks. See "Using 3.5-inch Floppy Disks," p. 120.

double-spin Describes CD-ROM drives that spin the disk twice as quickly as standard CD-ROM drives, so data can be read faster. See "CD-ROM," p. 126.

download To transfer files from another computer to your computer via a modem. See "Telecommunications," p. 32.

DPI Abbreviation for dots per inch, a measure of image resolution. See "Laser Printers," p. 170.

DR DOS An operating system that emulates the functions of MS-DOS. See "DOS," p. 204.

draw program A program that lets you draw pictures made up of lines and curves. See "Painting and Drawing," p. 30.

drum The rotating cylinder at the core of a laser printer. See "Laser Printers," p. 170.

DSR Abbreviation for Data Set Ready, the line of a serial I/O connection that the device uses to indicate that it is on and ready. See "Serial Ports," p. 158.

DTR Abbreviation for Data Terminal Ready, the line of a serial I/O connection that the computer uses to indicate that it is on and ready. See "Serial Ports," p. 158.

e-mail See *electronic mail.*

EGA Abbreviation for Enhanced Graphics Adapter, a mid-quality standard for video adapters. See "What Happens When You Use Your Monitor?" p. 142.

EISA Abbreviation for Extended Industry Standard Architecture, a standard design for system buses. See "The System Bus," p. 52.

electronic mail Letters and other documents sent via networks, information services, or bulletin board systems. See "Telecommunications," p. 32.

electrons Negatively charged subatomic particles. See "How Monitors Work," p. 144.

encoder wheel A wheel inside a mouse which is used to measure the speed and direction of the mouse's movement. See "The Mouse," p. 88.

enhancement technology The variation of the size of dots printed by laser printers, to create sharper images. See "Laser Printers," p. 170.

EtherNet A set of cabling and protocol standards for local area networks. See "The Physical Network," p. 196.

even parity One of two methods of calculating a parity bit value. See "Serial Ports," p. 158.

excited Used to describe phosphorous that has been exposed to electrons. See "Pixels and Resolution," p. 146.

executive word processor A word processing program with a limited but easy-to-use set of abilities. See "Word Processing," p. 22.

expanded memory A system of flipping different 16-kilobyte chunks of memory into and out of the 640K addressing space to which DOS is limited. See "DOS," p. 204.

extended density Describes floppy disks that can store more than high density disks. See "Using 3.5-inch Floppy Disks, p. 120.

extended memory RAM memory beyond the first megabyte. See "DOS," p. 204.

external modem A modem that sits outside of the computer, attached via a serial port. See "Types of Modems," p. 178.

FAT The File Allocation Table, which is used to keep track of which clusters on a disk are used and which are available. See "Sections of the Disk," p. 100.

fault line A line on a parallel I/O connection used by the device to tell the computer when something has gone wrong. See "Parallel Ports," p. 156.

fax modem A modem which communicates with fax machines. See "Types of Modems," p. 178.

female connector A connector socket. See "Parallel Ports," p. 156.

file A document, program, or other grouping of information stored on a disk. See "What Happens When Files Are Created?" p. 94.

file allocation table See *FAT*.

file area The portion of the disk used to store files. See "Sections of the Disk," p. 100.

file compression utility See *archive utility*.

file extension Characters at the end of a file name generally used to indicate what type of file it is. See "Types of Files," p. 96.

file server A computer which maintains and distributes the essential files on a local area network. See "What Happens When You Connect to a Local Area Network?" p. 194.

file transfer protocol A system of communications that ensures that information going from one computer to another is properly transmitted and understood. See "Transfer Protocols," p. 182.

fixed disk See *hard disk*.

flatbed plotter A type of plotter where the paper lies flat and still. See "Plotters," p. 172.

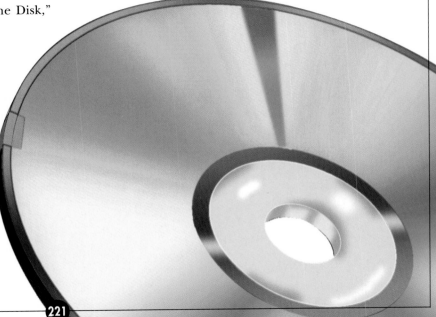

flatbed scanner A scanner in which the scanning of the page is automated. See "Hand Scanners and Flatbed Scanners," p. 188.

flight simulator A program that lets you simulate the experience of piloting an airplane. See "Games," p. 34.

Floating-point unit A special processor (called a math coprocessor) section of a processor designed specifically to handle complex math calculations quickly. Abbreviated FPU. See "The Central Processing Unit," p. 46.

floppy disk A magnetic disk in a covering jacket which is used to store information. See "Using 5.25-inch Floppy Disks," p. 118.

floptical A disk drive which reads and writes information magnetically, but uses light to help keep the read/write head on track. See "Optical Disks," p. 128.

font A design of type in a specific size. See "Daisywheel Printers," p. 164.

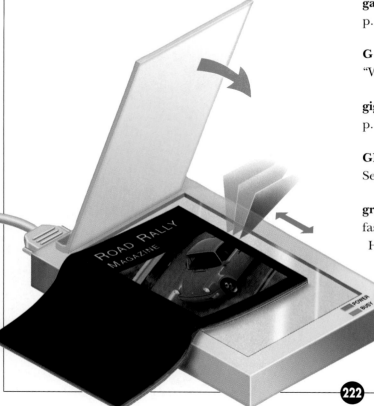

footprint The amount of space that a computer or peripheral takes up on the surface on which it is placed. See "The Keyboard," p. 86.

foreground Describes the program in a multitasking system to which keyboard input goes. See "What Is Multitasking?," p. 210.

formatting Preparing a disk so that it can store files. See "What Happens When You Format a Disk?" p. 134.

FPU See *floating-point unit.*

fragmented A condition where the files on a disk are broken up over many noncontiguous clusters. See "Fragmented Files," p. 108.

frequency The measurement of rate of waves or cycles. See "Modulation," p. 180.

function keys Numbered keys which are used differently by different programs. See "The Keyboard," p. 86.

game adapter An expansion board which provides game ports. See "Joysticks," p. 90.

game port Connection for a joystick. See "Joysticks," p. 90.

GeoWorks An operating environment. See "Windows," p. 206.

gigabyte 1,024 megabytes. See "Using Hard Drives," p. 122.

GND The ground wire in a serial I/O connection. See "Serial Ports," p. 158.

graphic accelerator A video adapter designed for faster processing of display information. See "What Happens When You Use Your Monitor?" p. 142.

graphic adapter See *video adapter.*

graphical user interface A system of communicating with a user using images as well as text. Abbreviated GUI. See "Windows," p. 206.

gray scale The number of different shades of gray that a scanner can interpret. See "Hand Scanners and Flatbed Scanners," p. 188.

ground An electrical line used to provide a base voltage necessary to complete a circuit. See "Parallel Ports," p. 156.

GUI See *graphical user interface.*

hammer pin The solenoid device which slams a printer's character arm against the ribbon. See "Daisywheel Printers," p. 164.

hand scanner A manually operated scanner. See "Hand Scanners and Flatbed Scanners," p. 188.

hard disk A disk drive designed to store a large amount of information. See "Using Hard Drives," p. 122.

head actuator The device which moves the read/write heads of a hard disk drive. See "Using Hard Drives," p. 122.

hertz Cycles per second, a measure of frequency. Abbreviated Hz. See "Scanning Frequency," p. 150.

hexadecimal A numbering system which uses a single character to represent each four bits. See "What Are Binary Numbers?" p. 12.

high-density Describes floppy disks coated in a way to be able to store more data than double-density disks. See "Using 5.25-inch Floppy Disks," p. 118.

high-level formatting Putting onto a disk the information and indexes that a given operating system needs to be able to keep the disk organized.

horizontal scanning frequency How long it takes the cathode ray tube to fire electrons across one row of screen pixels. See "Scanning Frequency," p. 150.

hub The central computer or device in a star configuration local area network. See "The Physical Network," p. 196.

Hz See *hertz.*

I/O Abbreviation for input/output. See "What Happens When You Use Your I/O Ports?" p. 154.

I/O controller An expansion card or set of chips on the motherboard which control passing information to the I/O ports. See "What Happens When You Use Your I/O Ports?" p. 154.

I/O device A device that can exchange information with the computer. See "I/O Devices," p. 56.

I/O ports Standard ports to which to connect input/output devices. See "What Happens When You Use Your I/O Ports?" p. 154.

IBMBIO.COM One of the essential files of PC DOS. See "DOS," p. 204.

IBMDOS.COM One of the essential files of PC DOS. See "DOS," p. 204.

icon A little picture used to represent a function or file. See "Windows," p. 206.

IDE Abbreviation for Integrated Drive Electronics, a standard for communicating between the disk controller and the disk drive. See "What Happens When You Use Your Disk Drives?" p. 116.

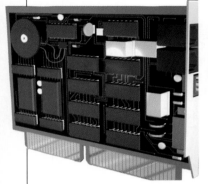

impact printer A printer which puts ink on the page by slamming character-shaping elements against an inked ribbon, which hits the paper. See "Daisywheel Printers," p. 164.

index hole A hole cut through the disc and jacket of a 5.25-inch floppy disk, which allows the computer to find the start of the disk. See "Using 5.25-inch Floppy Disks," p. 118.

init line A line in a parallel I/O connection which is used to reset the device to its initial state. See "Parallel Ports," p. 156.

inkjet printer A nonimpact printer which creates images by spraying ink dots onto the paper. See "Inkjet Printers," p. 168.

input The process of giving information to the computer, or the information that is given. See "What Is a Computer?" p. 8.

Installation program A program that sets up your system to be able to run a piece of software. See "The Operating System Adapts to You," p. 72.

instruction prefetch Part of a processor that gets commands from memory before they need to be executed. See "The Central Processing Unit," p. 46.

insulator A material that does not let energy pass through it easily. See "Transistor Switches," p. 42.

interlace A system of refreshing alternate lines of a monitor. See "Scanning Frequency," p. 150.

interleave factor How many sectors are skipped for each sector written to or read from an interleaved disk. See "Formatting Hard Disks," p. 138.

interleaving A system of storing data on disk sectors that are not right next to each other, which in some cases can increase disk speed. See "Formatting Hard Disks," p. 138.

internal modem A modem which installs in an expansion slot. See "Types of Modems," p. 178.

interpreter A program that takes a program written in a programming language and turns it, command by command, into machine language, and then immediately executes the machine language version. See "What Is a Computer Program," p. 16.

IO.SYS One of the essential files of MS-DOS. See "DOS," p. 204.

iron oxide A compound used to coat the disc of floppy disks, because it holds data easily. See "Using 5.25-inch Floppy Disks," p. 118.

ISA Abbreviation for Industry Standard Architecture, a standard design for the system bus. See "The System Bus," p. 52.

joystick An input device that lets you indicate a direction by tilting a stick in that direction. See "Joysticks," p. 90.

K See *kilobyte*.

KB See *kilobyte*.

kermit A file transfer protocol. See "Transfer Protocols," p. 182.

keyboard An array of buttons that lets the user type information into the computer. See "The Keyboard," p. 86.

keystroke buffer An area of RAM that stores the keys which have been pressed that the program has not yet had a chance to process. See "Input Devices," p. 84.

kHz See *kilohertz.*

kilobit 1,024 bits. See "Random-Access Memory," p. 48.

kilobyte 1,024 bytes. Abbreviated K or KB. See "Random-Access Memory," p. 48.

kilohertz A measure of thousands of cycles per second. Abbreviated kHz. See "Scanning Frequency," p. 150.

label Text information in a spreadsheet cell. See "Doing Math," p. 28.

LAN See *local area network.*

land A flat area on a CD-ROM disk. See "CD-ROM," p. 126.

laptop computer A computer designed to be easily carried around. See "Basic Computer Anatomy," p. 38.

laser printer A nonimpact printer in which a laser creates a static image of the page on a rotating drum, which then collects toner on the statically charged portions and delivers it to the page. See "Laser Printers," p. 170.

LED Abbreviation for light emitting diode. A small electronic device which lights up when electricity flows through it in a given direction. See "Using 3.5-inch Floppy Disks," p. 120.

light pen A wand which, when touched to the screen, can detect which location on the screen it is touching. See "Input Devices," p. 84.

line noise Interference and other stray sounds on a communication line. See "Transfer Protocols," p. 182.

loading Copying a program from a disk into RAM. See "What Happens When You Load a Program?" p. 76.

local area network A system of cabling together a number of computers, allowing them to share information. Abbreviated LAN. See "What Happens When You Connect to a Local Area Network?" p. 194.

local bus A direct high-speed connection between the CPU and RAM, and other peripherals. See "The System Bus," p. 52.

local bus adapter An adapter card which attaches to the local bus. See "What Happens When You Use Your Monitor?" p. 142.

local bus graphic accelerator A graphic accelerator that attaches to the local bus. See "What Happens When You Use Your Monitor?" p. 142.

logical operators The different types of comparisons that are possible in binary logic. See "Binary Logic," p. 14.

16 COLORS

mechanical keyboard A keyboard where pressing the key separates electrical contacts. See "The Keyboard," p. 86.

mechanical mouse A mouse whose movement is measured by the turning of an encoder wheel across electrical contacts. See "The Mouse," p. 88.

membrane keyboard A keyboard where pressing the key pushes electrical contacts together. See "The Keyboard," p. 86.

meg See *megabyte.*

megabit 1,048,576 bits. See "Random-Access Memory," p. 48.

megabyte 1,048,576 bytes. Abbreviated MB or meg. See "Random-Access Memory," p. 48.

millisecond A thousandth of a second. See "Using Hard Drives," p. 122.

modem A device that allows computers to communicate with each other over phone lines. See "What Happens When You Use Your Modem," p. 176.

modulate To vary sound, or to adapt. A modem does both in encoding information as sound. See "Modulation," p. 180.

monitor A TV-like information display. See "What Happens When You Use Your Monitor?" p. 142.

motherboard The printed circuit board where the main electronics of the computer reside. See "The Motherboard," p. 44.

mouse An input device which is controlled by sliding it across a flat surface. See "The Mouse," p. 88.

MS-DOS An operating system produced by Microsoft Corporation. See "DOS," p. 204.

low-level formatting Raking out the tracks and marking the sectors on a disk. See "What Happens When You Format a Disk?" p. 134.

machine language The command language that the processor can directly understand. See "Scanning Frequency," p. 150.

magneto-optical drives Disk drives which store and read information using a combination of magnetism and light. See "Optical Disks," p. 128.

mail merge A word processing feature that lets you take information from a series of database records into a fixed form. See "Keeping Records," p. 26.

male connector A connector with exposed pins or leads that slides into a female connector socket. See "Parallel Ports," p. 156.

matrix A grid. See "Dot-Matrix Printers," p. 166.

MB See *megabyte.*

MCA Abbreviation for Micro-Channel Architecture, an IBM-generated standard design for system buses. See "The System Bus," p. 52.

MSDOS.SYS One of the essential files of MS-DOS. See "DOS," p. 204.

Multiscan monitor A monitor that can accept and display data at more than one display frequency. See "Scanning Frequency," p. 150.

multisession Describes a CD-ROM drive that supports a special directory format which allows information to be added to a disk by special devices designed for that purpose. See "CD-ROM," p. 126.

multitasking A system of running more than one program on a computer, seemingly simultaneously. See "What Is Multitasking?," p. 210.

multithreading Running more than one chain of commands in a single program, seemingly simultaneously. See "What Is Multitasking?," p. 210.

NAND A logical operator that puts out a true (or 1) value if either of the values going in are false (or 0). See "Binary Logic," p. 14.

nanosecond A billionth of a second. See "Random-Access Memory," p. 48.

near letter quality An operating mode of dot-matrix printers which achieves sharper-looking characters by making multiple passes across each line. Abbreviated NLQ. See "Dot-Matrix Printers," p. 166.

network interface card An expansion card which allows a computer to hook up to a local area network. See "The Physical Network," p. 196.

Nike network A nickname for the practice of regularly transferring files from computer to computer on floppy disks. See "What Happens When You Connect to a Local Area Network?" p. 194.

NLQ See *near letter quality.*

non-impact printer A printer which forms characters without striking the paper. See "Inkjet Printers," p. 168.

NOR A logical operator that puts out a true (or 1) value only if both of the values going in are false (or 0). See "Binary Logic," p. 14.

NOT A logical operator that puts out the opposite value of what is put in. See "Binary Logic," p. 14 .

Novell DOS An operating system that emulates the functions of MS-DOS. See "DOS," p. 204.

null modem cable A cable that allows you to connect to computer serial ports directly, so it will appear to the computers as if they are connected via a modem. See "Serial Ports," p. 158.

nybble Half a byte. (Also spelled *nybble.*) See "What Are Binary Numbers," p. 12.

OCR Abbreviation for Optical Character Recognition, a system of translating scanned text into a form that the computer can understand as text. See "Optical Character Recognition," p. 190.

odd parity One of two methods of calculating a parity bit value. See "Serial Ports," p. 158.

operating environment A program system which provides tools in addition to the ones built into the operating system. See "Windows," p. 206.

operating system A series of programs designed to handle many of the essential processes of the computer. Abbreviated OS. See "What Happens When You Use an Operating System?" p. 202.

optical drives Disk drives which write or read information using light. See "Optical Disks," p. 128.

optical mouse A mouse where the movement is measured by light bouncing off of a gridded pad under the mouse. See "The Mouse," p. 88.

opti-mechanical mouse A mouse where the movement is measured by light passing through slots in a rotating wheel. See "The Mouse," p. 88.

optimizer See *defragmenter*.

OR A logical operator that puts out a true (or 1) value if either of the values going in are true (or 1). See "Binary Logic," p. 14.

OS See *operating system*.

OS/2 A multitasking, multithreading operating system produced by IBM. See "OS/2," p. 212.

output The process of getting information out of a computer, or the information that comes out. See "What Is a Computer?" p. 8.

overlay Pieces of a program that can be loaded into and out of memory separately from the main program. See "Loading Pieces of Programs," p. 80.

packet A group of characters transferred from one computer to another, including control information. See "Transfer Protocols," p. 182.

page description language A printer command language which includes the ability to describe an entire page as groups of objects. Abbreviated PDL. See "Laser Printers," p. 170.

page printers Printers which print a whole page as a single action, rather than a single character or single line. See "Laser Printers," p. 170.

paint program A program that lets you draw pictures by setting the colors of pixels. See "Painting and Drawing," p. 30.

palette The colors that can be chosen for a computer image. See "Available Colors," p. 148.

paper out line A line in a parallel port connection used by printers to announce when they are out of paper. See "Parallel Ports," p. 156.

parallel port A connector that can exchange data with an I/O device eight bits at a time. See "Parallel Ports," p. 156.

parity bit A calculated bit used to check the integrity of a character of data. See "Random-Access Memory," p. 48.

partition A group of cylinders of a hard disk which appears to the system to be a single, separate disk drive. See "Formatting Hard Disks," p. 138.

PC See *personal computer*.

PC DOS A version of the DOS operating system produced by IBM. See "DOS," p. 204.

PDL See *page description language*.

personal computer A small computer designed for a single user. Abbreviated PC.

phase The spacing between two similar waves. See "Modulation," p. 180.

phosphorous A chemical that glows when struck by electrons. See "How Monitors Work," p. 144.

pit A small area dug out of a CD-ROM disk. See "CD-ROM," p. 126.

pixel A small rectangle which is the smallest possible piece of a graphic image. See "Pixels and Resolution," p. 146.

platen The cushioned cylinder that paper wraps around in some printers. See "Daisywheel Printers," p. 164.

platen knob A knob that allows you to turn the platen manually. See "Daisywheel Printers," p. 164.

platters Individual disks of hard disk media. See "Using Hard Drives," p. 122.

plotter A type of printer which draws lines on the page with a pen. See "Plotters," p. 172.

pointer A user-controlled screen image which points to things. See "Windows," p. 206.

POST Abbreviation for Power On Self Test, a series of checks that the computer runs through when turned on to make sure that everything is working okay. See "The Computer Checks Itself," p. 66.

power supply A device inside the computer which regulates and distributes the electricity for the computer's internal components. See "The Power System," p. 60.

PPM Abbreviation for pages per minute, a measure of printer speed. See "Laser Printers," p. 170.

preemptive multitasking A system of multitasking that does not require the programs to voluntarily pass processor control on to the next program. See "What Is Multitasking?," p. 210.

Presentation Manager A user interface system in OS/2. See "OS/2," p. 212.

print head The portion of some printers that slides along the page, putting the characters on the paper. See "Daisywheel Printers," p. 164.

printer An output device which puts information on paper. See "What Happens When You Use Your Printer?" p. 162.

printer driver A small program designed to allow another program to communicate with a specific brand and model of printer. See "Loading Pieces of Programs," p. 80.

printer ribbon A long strip of fabric saturated with ink, used in impact printers. See "Daisywheel Printers," p. 164.

processor A chip that processes commands. See also *Central processing unit.*

professional word processing program A word processing program with a full range of functions. See "Word Processing," p. 22.

program A list of computer commands designed to perform a specific function. See "What Is a Computer Program?" p. 16.

program file A file which stores a program. See "Types of Files," p. 96.

programming language Any of a number of systems for describing commands to the computer. See "What Is a Computer Program?" p. 16.

quick format A method of clearing information from a disk without actually reformatting it. See "Formatting Floppy Disks," p. 136.

RAM See *random-access memory.*

RAM disk An area of RAM set aside to store files. See "RAM Disks," p. 130.

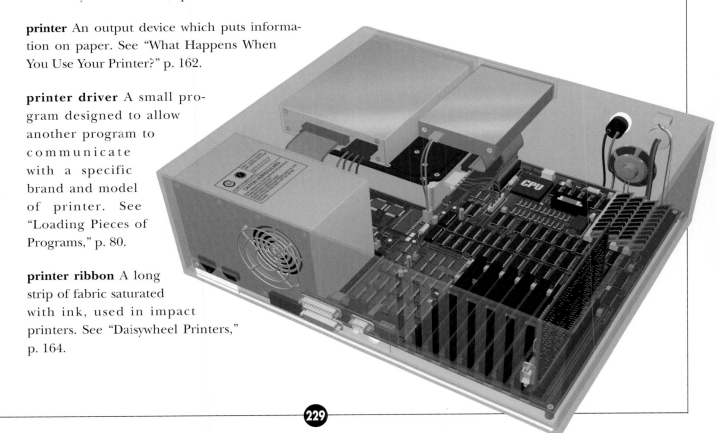

Random-access memory Memory chips that store information that can be easily read or written to. Abbreviated RAM. See "Random-Access Memory," p. 48.

range the total number of different colors that a video adapter can support. See "Available Colors," p. 148.

Read-only memory Information storage that cannot be changed by the standard computer. Abbreviated ROM. See "Read-Only Memory," p. 50.

read/write head The part of a disk drive that actually reads and writes the information on the disk. See "Using 5.25-inch Floppy Disks," p. 118.

record A single entry of information in a database. See "Keeping Records," p. 26.

registers Special data storage locations on a processor. See "The Central Processing Unit," p. 46.

regular density Describes floppy disks with a coating able to hold the minimum amount of data. See "Using 5.25-inch Floppy Disks," p. 118.

removable hard disk A special sort of hard disk where the platters and some of the mechanism is removable. See "Using Hard Drives," p. 122.

repeater A device which can serve as a hub of a local area network. See "The Physical Network," p. 196.

resolution The density of dots that is used to make up an image. See "Pixels and Resolution," p. 146.

RI Abbreviation for ring indicator, the line in a serial modem connection used to indicate that the phone is ringing. See "Serial Ports," p. 158.

ribbon cartridge A plastic casing which holds a printer ribbon. See "Daisywheel Printers," p. 164.

RISC Abbreviation for Reduced Instruction Set Computing, a processor design philosophy that focuses on being able to handle a few instructions quickly. See "The Central Processing Unit," p. 46.

ROM See *Read-only memory.*

root directory The first directory on a disk. See "How Directories Are Organized," p. 98.

RTS Abbreviation for request to send, the line on a serial I/O connection that the computer uses to let the device know that it is ready to accept data. See "Serial Ports," p. 158.

RX The line in a serial I/O connection on which the device transmits data. See "Serial Ports," p. 158.

scanner A device which transfers paper images into the computer. See "What Happens When You Use Your Scanner?" p. 186.

scanning frequency How quickly the electron beam passes across the screen. See "Scanning Frequency," p. 150.

screen mode A display format supported by a video adapter, defined by the resolution, the number of colors it supports, and whether it expects information as text or as graphics. See "Pixels and Resolution," p. 146.

SCSI Abbreviation for Small Computer Standard Interface, a standard for communicating between a controller and disk drives and other devices. See "What Happens When You Use Your Disk Drives?" p. 116.

sector An arc-shaped section of a disk. See "Sections of the Disk," p. 100.

sector header An area at the beginning of a sector which contains the sector number. See "Formatting Floppy Disks," p. 136.

segment A 64 kilobyte chunk of memory. See "DOS," p. 204.

select button A printer control button which allows you to take it on-line and off-line. See "Daisywheel Printers," p. 164.

select input line A line in a parallel I/O connection used by the computer to control whether the device is on-line. See "Parallel Ports," p. 156.

select line A line in a parallel I/O connection used to tell the computer whether the printer is on-line or off-line. See "Parallel Ports," p. 156.

serial port A connector that lets the computer exchange information with an I/O device one bit at a time. See "Serial Ports," p. 158.

shadow mask A filter inside the cathode ray tube of a color monitor that directs the electron streams toward the proper colors of phosphorous dots. See "How Monitors Work," p. 144.

shadowing Copying the BIOS from ROM to RAM, to make it run faster. See "The Basic Input/Output System," p. 68.

sheet feeder A device which loads individual pieces of paper into a printer. See "Daisywheel Printers," p. 164.

side The top or bottom of an individual platter or disc in a disk drive. See "What Happens When You Format a Disk?" p. 134.

silicon The primary element of the construction of transistors. See "Transistor Switches," p. 42.

SIMM Abbreviation for Single In-Line Memory Module, a board with RAM chips on it designed to fit into a standard slot. See "Random-Access Memory," p. 48.

sneakernet A nickname for the practice of regularly transferring files from computer to computer on floppy disks. See "What Happens When You Connect to a Local Area Network?" p. 194.

soft formatting See *high level formatting*.

solenoid A magnetically controlled two-position electric device. See "Dot-Matrix Printers," p. 166.

sound digitizer A device which turns a sound into computer data that can be used to re-create the sound. See "Input Devices," p. 84.

space-saver keyboard See *compact keyboard*.

sports simulation A game program designed to represent a popular sport. See "Games," p. 34.

spreadsheet A calculation program that lets you lay out numbers and equations on a grid, in a way that makes it easy to change the numbers and recalculate. See "Doing Math," p. 28.

star configuration A local area network layout which involves each computer talking directly with a central hub. See "The Physical Network," p. 196.

start bit A bit sent to indicate the start of a character in a serial communication. See "Serial Ports," p. 158.

Red Separation

stop bit A bit sent to indicate the end of a character in a serial communication. See "Serial Ports," p. 158.

Green Separation

stress relief notch Small holes cut out of the edge of a 5.25-inch floppy disk to prevent warping. See "Using 5.25-inch Floppy Disks," p. 118.

subdirectory A directory which exists as part of another directory. See "How Directories Are Organized," p. 98.

Blue Separation

super VGA A video adapter that goes beyond the VGA standard. See "What Happens When You Use Your Monitor?" p. 142.

support file A file that a program needs in addition to the program file. See "Types of Files," p. 96.

surge protector A device that plugs in between the computer plug and the power socket, that is designed to protect the computer from damage from bad electrical lines. "The Power System," p. 60.

system area The portion of the disk devoted to organizing the disk structure. See "Sections of the Disk," p. 100.

system board See *motherboard*.

system bus The series of electronic wiring and adapter slots that allows the processor to communicate with most peripherals. See "The System Bus," p. 52.

system disk A disk that has the operating system on it, and therefore can be used to start the system. See "Formatting Floppy Disks," p. 136.

templates Premade page designs for word processing or desktop publishing programs. See "Desktop Publishing," p. 24.

text mode A mode of display or interface that works without graphics. See "OS/2," p. 212.

thin ethernet A cabling standard for local area networks. See "The Physical Network," p. 196.

time slicing Dividing the processor time over several different programs, giving each a limited amount of time before moving on to the next one. See "What Is Multitasking?" p. 210.

toner A fine black powder which takes the place of liquid ink in laser printers. See "Laser Printers," p. 170.

touch screen A monitor with the built-in ability to detect where on the computer a user's finger is touching. See "Input Devices," p. 84.

tower computer A computer designed to stand on the floor, generally next to a desk. See "Basic Computer Anatomy," p. 38.

track A single circular path on one side of a disk. See "What Happens When You Format a Disk?" p. 134.

trackball An input device where the user rolls the top of a ball with his hand. See "The Mouse," p. 88.

tractor feed A system of pulling paper through a printer, which requires paper with a series of holes along the edges. See "Dot-Matrix Printers," p. 166.

transistor A switch-like electronic device that lets electrical current pass through only if a specific charge is applied to it. See "Transistor Switches," p. 42.

triple-spin Describes a CD-ROM drive which spins the disk at three times the standard rate, allowing the information to be read more quickly. See "CD-ROM," p. 126.

true color Used to describe video adapters that support so large a range of colors that they can display pictures which are indistinguishable from a TV display. See "Available Colors," p. 148.

twisted-pair cable A type of cable with pairs of intertwined wires running through it, twisted together. See "The Physical Network," p. 196.

TX The line in a serial I/O connection that the computer transmits data on. See "Serial Ports," p. 158.

undelete To recover a deleted file. See "Deleting a File," p. 106.

uninterruptible power supply A device designed to continue providing power to the computer when the standard electrical supply fails. Abbreviated UPS. See "The Power System," p. 60.

upload To transfer files from your computer to another computer over a modem. See "Telecommunications," p. 32.

UPS See *uninterruptible power supply.*

variable resistor An electrical device which lets a different amount of power pass through, depending where on the device the electrical contact is made. See "Joysticks," p. 90.

VDU Video display unit. See *monitor.*

vertical scanning frequency How quickly the monitor can refresh the entire screen. See "Scanning Frequency," p. 150.

VGA Abbreviation for Video Graphics Array, a high-quality standard for video adapters. See "What Happens When You Use Your Monitor?" p. 142.

video adapter A board or set of chips used to process screen information and relay it to the monitor. See "What Happens When You Use Your Monitor," p. 142.

virtual disk See *RAM disk.*

virtual machine A set of memory and processes that function as an entire separate computer. See "Windows," p. 206.

voice recognition A system designed to understand the human voice. See "Input Devices," p. 84.

warm boot Reinitializing a computer without turning it off first. See "Finding the Operating System," p. 70.

WIMP An abbreviation for Windows, icons, mouse, and pointer. A description of the elements that make up most graphical user interfaces. See "Windows," p. 206.

window A rectangular area on the screen used to convey information associated with a specific program or function. See "Windows," p. 206.

Windows A popular operating environment. See "Windows," p. 206.

wireless network system A local area network where the computers communicate via radio waves instead of via cables. See "The Physical Network," p. 196.

word processing program A program that lets you create and change reports, letters, and other text documents. See "Word Processing," p. 22.

worksheet The document created and edited with a spreadsheet program. See "Doing Math," p. 28.

WORM Abbreviation for Write Once/Read Mostly. Describes a disk where information cannot be erased or written over once written. See "Optical Disks," p. 128.

write enable notch A hole cut into a 5.25-inch floppy disk drive, that is used to indicate to the drive that this disk can be written to. See "Using 5.25-inch Floppy Disks," p. 118.

write protect switch A switch built into a 3.5-inch floppy disk which lets the disk drive know whether it is okay to write to the disk. See "Using 3.5-inch Floppy Disks," p. 120.

wxmodem A file transfer protocol. See "Transfer Protocols," p. 182.

X-axis The line along which side-to-side position is measured. See "Joysticks," p. 90.

XGA Abbreviation for Extended Graphics Array, a very high standard for video adapters. See "What Happens When You Use Your Monitor?" p. 142.

xmodem A file transfer protocol. See "Transfer Protocols," p. 182.

XOR A logical operator that puts out a true (or 1) value only if one but not both of the values going in are true (or 1). See "Binary Logic," p. 14.

Y-axis The line along which front-to-back or vertical position is measured. See "Joysticks," p. 90.

ymodem A file transfer protocol. See "Transfer Protocols," p. 182.

zmodem A file transfer protocol. See "Transfer Protocols," p. 182.

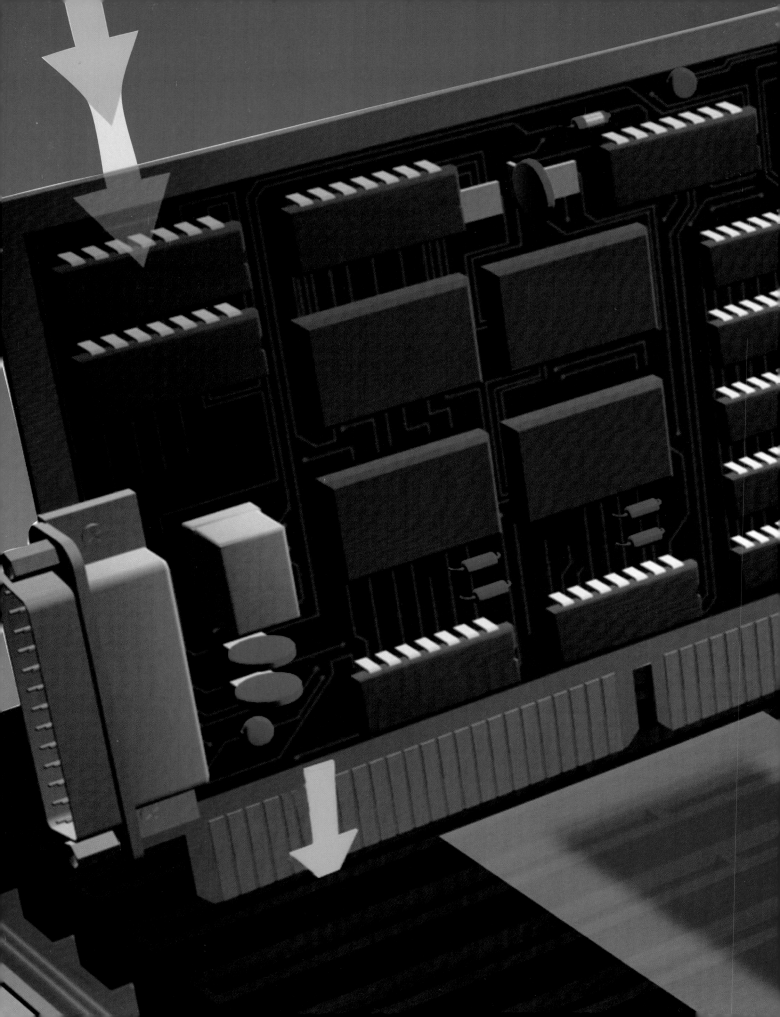

INDEX

E

F

G